Adventurers Abroad

Ruby,

Thanks for a
really excellent
job decorating
Articles for me.
The very best to
you in your life
Abroad.

Best,

Bob

Adventurers Abroad

The New American Expat Generation

Robert Nelson

For Felice, my muse and my love.

Table of Contents

Introduction

In 2013, two hundred and thirty-two million people, or just over three percent of the world's population, were living outside of their country of origin. The United Nations, which tracks international migration annually, reported that migration from one country to another is a global phenomenon that is growing in scope, complexity and impact, and is a modern reality of a globalized world.

Taken together, this migrant population would be the fifth largest country in the world and is growing at a current rate of nearly one and a half percent a year.

World migration population statistics include a wide range of migrants who move for better employment opportunities, asylum, tax avoidance, adventure and a host of other reasons. Less than seven percent are classified as refugees.

Where are these migrants heading? Europe and Asia combined hold nearly two-thirds of all international migrants worldwide, with seventy-two million calling Europe home and an almost equal amount found in Asia.

About fifty-one percent of all international migrants in the world live in just ten countries. The United States attracts the most, followed by the Russian Federation, Germany, Saudi Arabia, the United Arab Emirates, the United Kingdom, France, Canada, Australia and Spain.

Robert Nelson

The United Nations considers anyone, regardless of socio-economic factors, to be an international migrant if they move from one country to another, whether or not they intend to stay permanently or acquire citizenship. International migrants can be called immigrants or expatriates.

As you will see later in this book, a few of our expat adventurers might be termed immigrants to their new homeland because they married citizens of the country and acquired citizenship themselves, with no intent to return home.

The most common definition of an expatriate, however, is anyone who lives outside of his or her nation of origin for at least six months of any twelve-month period.

Merriam-Webster, on the other hand, defines expatriate in more pejorative terms: "To withdraw (oneself) from residence in or allegiance to one's native country." The idea of renouncing allegiance to your country has been the way expatriates have been viewed historically.

The contemporary interpretation of expatriate, though, is rooted more in the notion of choosing to live abroad, without renouncing citizenship.

In America, the first use of the term expatriate was Lillian Bell's early twentieth- century novel, "The Expatriates." Many Americans seem to associate the word expatriate with the romantic "Lost Generation" of writers and artists who flocked to Paris in the nineteen-twenties. Hemingway, F. Scott Fitzgerald, Gertrude Stein and other creative souls gave legitimacy to being an expat for reasons other than immigrating to another country, although even they believed the term expatriate had a negative undertone that questioned their fealty to America.

By the mid-twentieth century, global mobility and economic globalization began to change our understanding of expatriate to mean someone

sent abroad to work for a multinational company. Today, an expat is someone living abroad permanently or for a specific period of time for a wide
range of reasons.

Globalization, modern technology and transportation improvements
have literally shrunk the world we live in, and those changes are reflected
in the large and growing number of American expats.

The U.S. Department of State's latest estimate in 2013 of the number
of Americans living abroad was nearly seven million, about a half million
more than in July 2012. There were only four million Americans living in
other countries in 1999. The government data exclude U.S. military and non-
military government employees. To put these numbers in perspective, the
American expat community would be our country's fourteenth largest state.

The number of Americans living abroad is about three percent of all
international migrants in the world and is the subject of this book.

My wife Felice and I are both former expats, she in London and I in Puerto
Vallarta, Mexico. Our interest in the lives of expats led us to create myinterna-
tionaladventure.com, an online guide for aspiring American expats.

Before we launched our website several years ago, we spent a great deal
of time researching expats and learning about their needs and wants to
better prepare them for their new lives abroad.

Our research, and other studies we consulted, turned up an interesting
finding, which is the focus of this book. We discovered a new American
expat generation that is younger, well educated, entrepreneurial and actively looking for adventure and opportunities abroad.

The first chapter of this book describes the new American expat generation, a new class of truly world citizens. You will learn whom they are,

why they become expats, where they live and other dimensions of this new generation of expats.

The following chapters will introduce you to fourteen members of the new American expat generation, who will tell you about their own personal stories of life abroad. From the peripatetic entrepreneur in Mexico and Argentina to the research scientist in France, you will see why expat life is such an adventure.

The last chapter takes a look at the key characteristics experts and adventurers believe you will need to become a successful expat and a member of the new American expat generation.

CHAPTER 1

The New American
Expat Generation

WE LIVE IN an age of economic globalization and global mobility where increasingly advanced communication technology and an interconnected world transportation system enable fluid movement between countries. Unlike the "Lost Generation" of American expatriates in early twentieth-century Paris, expats today can easily live almost anywhere in the world, and do.

The twenty-first century is creating a new class of expats, world citizens who are at ease living abroad and often move from country to country to find new adventures, experiences and opportunities.

In 2002, I moved to Puerto Vallarta, Mexico, a place I had visited often and always loved. I was able to live there because it had an international airport with many direct flights to the United States, was just a few hours away from most major U.S. cities and had a telecommunications infrastructure that supported the communication I required for my brand consulting practice.

I found I was not alone. As I began researching my book, *Boomers in Paradise: Living in Puerto Vallarta*, I discovered many American and Canadian expats who operated similar businesses, some focused primarily on U.S. customers and others on international clientele. I also found that many worked locally or had their own businesses. But most importantly, I found that many of them had moved to Puerto Vallarta at a young age, often in their twenties and thirties and now were well integrated into the local community and spoke fluent Spanish.

When I returned to the San Francisco Bay Area in 2009 to resume teaching advertising at San Jose State University, my wife Felice – a former expat who lived in London for seven years – and I began researching the world of expats to learn more about the lives of those who choose to live abroad.

What we learned led us to the formation of MyInternationalAdventure LLC, an online publisher of international relocation information and resources to help aspiring American expats move, live and work abroad. We launched myinternationaladventure.com in January 2013 to serve the needs of what we called the new American expat generation.

Who Are They?

The U.S. Department of State's 2013 estimate of nearly seven million Americans living abroad was a seventy-five percent increase over its 1999 estimate of about four million. Considering that a number of expats repatriate each year, whether returning from an overseas assignment, returning home disillusioned with life abroad or coming home for another reason, the increase in the number of American expats over the past several decades has been strong.

We wanted to know, though, how many Americans were planning to move each year. That information was not available from U.S. government statistics.

So in 2011, we asked the San Francisco-based research firm Socratic Technologies to help us answer that question and many others we had about prospective American expats. The research firm interviewed over two hundred American adults who were twenty-five years of age or older and considering or planning a move abroad.

Our study found that – projecting statistically - over ten million Americans were considering or actively planning a move to another country that year.

Adventurers Abroad

The ten million represented about five percent of all Americans over the age of twenty-five. Over forty percent of them said they were extremely or very likely to move abroad, and about one-third said they would move within the next year.

We were surprised that about four million American adults said they were very likely to move abroad and looked for other research that might confirm the size of this new American expat generation.

We found that confirmation in seminal research done by New Global Initiatives, a Washington D.C.-based consulting firm. It had been conducting expat studies through its research firm, Zogby International, between 2005 and 2011. The initial study in 2005 sampled twenty-five thousand adults over the age of eighteen and found that the number of Americans who were planning a move abroad was well over three million people and steadily growing.

The most important discovery in the research done by MyInternationalAdventure and New Global Initiatives, though, was the age of the new American expat generation.

In our research, the over-sixty-five age group represented less than three percent of all aspiring expats, which was a surprise considering how many articles have been published by the media on Americans retiring abroad. The largest group we found fell between the ages of twenty-five and thirty-four, the older portion of the Millennial generation, born in the two decades before 2000. The older Millennials represented more than one-third of all those who said they were considering or planning a move abroad. The thirty-five to forty-four age group was second in size and also an important component of the new American expat generation.

The numbers were even more impressive in the New Global Initiatives studies. In 2007, about three and a half percent of all twenty-five to thirty-four-year-old adults said they planned to relocate abroad, but that number jumped to over five percent by 2011, meaning that over two million older Millennials were planning a move to another country. By comparison, in the 2011 study, just over two percent of Americans over the age of thirty-five were planning to relocate abroad.

The Millennial movement abroad soon could grow much larger, much faster. Younger Millennials – those between the ages of eighteen and twenty-four – often are constrained by the amount of money it takes to move abroad. But an increasing number of them are packing their bags and hitting the road, often teaching English in other countries and developing a taste for the expat lifestyle.

Add to that the very active student learning abroad programs found in most American universities and colleges, which expose young people to life in other countries, and you can easily see why the new American expat generation will continue to grow in the future. During the 2013 – 2014 academic year alone, nearly three hundred thousand U.S. students studied abroad.

As this younger Millennial group ages, we expect the new American expat generation to swell. As Bob Adams, the former CEO of New Global Initiatives and current owner of Panama-based America Wave – put it: "For one thing, younger people are far better traveled than any previous generation. And, because of globalization, they are exposed in school and through the news media to life in other countries. They also have peer communication with those who have traveled and lived abroad."

Results from the large London-based Expat Survey 2013, also agreed that America's youth is driving the new American expat generation.

i-World Research, the firm that conducted the study, received responses from about eight thousand expats in one hundred twenty-eight countries. Survey Director Emma Wood told us, "There is a youth element to moving abroad, particularly from America. Ten years ago Americans were not really up there, but that has changed in the last five years with the younger generation of Americans adopting a much more adventurous attitude. They are much more inquisitive about foreign cultures. Those below the age of thirty, in particular, have adopted the attitude: 'If I don't do it now, when am I going to do it?'"

Why Are They Moving Abroad?

What is motivating this new American expat generation to pick up and move abroad?

MyInternationalAdventure research showed that by far the strongest motivations centered on a desire for a sense of adventure and a need for new experiences. Much like the "Lost Generation," the new American expat generation is looking for something a little out of the ordinary.

Nearly half of the U.S. adults we surveyed said either they wanted a lifestyle change or wanted a new life adventure. About forty percent said they wanted to experience a new culture. But, nearly one-third said they were looking for a new business opportunity.

That is not surprising, since it is Millennials who are driving the growth of the new American expat generation.

Research by MyInternationalAdventure found that forty-one percent of older Millennials gave starting a new business as a key reason for moving abroad.

The Millennial generation is filled with entrepreneurs and risk takers who look for adventure. The most tech-savvy generation ever, Millennials are rightfully called digital natives because they were teethed on computers, the Internet and social media, all of which are necessary tools for success-ful twenty-first century businesses abroad.

The very large Expat Survey 2013 found that many Millennials have an entrepreneurial bent and are looking for opportunities abroad. The study showed that opportunity is particularly high for starting your own business in Southern Europe, particularly in Portugal, Spain, Italy and Croatia.

A survey by the consulting giant Deloitte in 2014 supports the idea of Millennials as entrepreneurs. It reported that roughly seventy percent of Millennials see themselves working independently at some point in their lives, rather than being employed within a traditional organization structure.

Another global consulting firm, Pricewaterhouse Cooper (PwC), con-ducted a global generational study in 2013 and remarked: "Millennials are particularly attuned to the world around them and many want the chance to explore overseas positions."

That same study also pointed out that, "The fundamental reason we can expect the Millennial generation to be different, and in a dramatically different way from previous generations, is the information revolution now unfolding and the explosion of possibilities this presents. These pos-sibilities are delivered by globalization. The influences penetrate societies in ways not previously possible."

The Millennial generation has proved to be the most entrepreneurial generation in modern times, more often shunning the corporate ladder to start new businesses.

Author and long-time *Inc. Magazine* contributing editor, Donna Fenn, explained why Millennials are taking to entrepreneurship like no other generation before them.

"Being an entrepreneur was not always viewed positively by previous generations, but this generation does not remember a time when entrepreneurs were not viewed as rock stars. Perceptions began to change in the 1980s when Steve Jobs, Michael Dell, Bill Gates, Richard Branson and others became very successful entrepreneur role models, and continues today with people like Facebook's Mark Zuckerberg."

Donna explained to me that among Millennials there is a basic distrust of institutions, whether its government or big companies. They have lived through corporate scandals and have watched their Baby Boomer generation parents being laid off after many years of service to big corporations, and know there is no longer such a thing as getting a gold watch after thirty years of service."

She related many stories of inventive young Millennial entrepreneurs abroad, including the story of a young man she had met in Uganda. "There was one fellow I met who started a company in Kampala after he observed a specific local market need. In Kampala, a common form of transportation is a motorcycle taxi driven by what they call 'bota bota' men. This young entrepreneur saw an opportunity to make local entrepreneurs out of these 'bota bota' men by offering them financing to buy their own vehicles. That is how he makes his money, by creating entrepreneurs in Uganda."

John Wennersten, the author of *Leaving America: The New Expatriate Generation*, agrees that many Millennials are striking out on their own to start businesses abroad. John told me that the new American expat generation is made up of high achievers, people familiar with information technology, marketing people and young entrepreneurs. He said, "Many younger people are moving to emerging countries to start businesses, which is particularly true of the Middle East, the Persian Gulf and Australia."

Robert Nelson

Where Are They Moving Abroad?

The nearly seven million American expats can be found scattered throughout the world, according to a 2013 U.S. Department of State estimate.

By region, the Western Hemisphere has almost two and a half million American expats residing in the lands from Canada to South America. Europe is second with just over one and a half million, followed by the Near East with just under one million. East Asia and Pacific, South Central Asia and Africa hold the remaining American expats.

That same U.S. Department of State estimate also said there were thirteen countries with more than one hundred thousand resident Americans: Australia, Canada, China, Dominican Republic, France, Germany, Greece, Israel, Italy, Mexico, the Philippines, Spain and the United Kingdom. Mexico alone hosts close to one million American expats.

But where is the new American expat generation headed? The MyInternationalAdventure study showed that the United Kingdom was the top choice for Americans considering a move to another country, by a fairly wide margin. A shared language and a high quality of life seem to add up to a place where many Americans want to live and work. Two other English-speaking countries, Canada and Australia, round out the top three most attractive countries for the new American expat generation.

France and Germany also are high on the list of places Americans want to move, ranking fourth and fifth. Europe as a region did well in the study.

Two countries south of America's border were next on the list of preferred locations. Eco-friendly Costa Rica was ranked sixth and expat haven Mexico was seventh.

Rounding out the top ten were Italy in eighth place, Switzerland in ninth and China in tenth place.

The Lives of the New American Expat Generation

Real understanding, though, best comes from hearing the stories of life lived abroad from the lips of the new American expat generation. The adventurer stories you will read in the next chapters of the book will give you a deep, personal sense of who these people are, what they care about, what they do everyday, where they live and how living abroad has changed their lives.

I think you will soon see that expats have a very different view of the world. From a serial entrepreneur in Mexico and Argentina to a research scientist in Marseilles, France, all share experiences that can only be known by adventurers abroad.

CHAPTER 2

Tony Bishop
Age 31
Buenos Aires, Argentina

"I did not want to do the same thing as my dad. He worked in a factory for thirty years before he finally retired and I did not want to do that. I found a university in Puebla that had the same accreditation as U.S. universities to pursue my master's degree. I sold all my furniture, rented out my house, sold pretty much everything, quit my job and moved to Mexico."

TONY BISHOP GETS bored easily. An ambitious, energetic and entrepreneurial young man, he has done more living before the age of thirty than most people experience in a lifetime.

Born and raised in the small southern Michigan town of Sturgis, Tony has always been restless and in a hurry. He left for college in Gola, Indiana one week before his high school graduation to start a full-time job in the hotel industry while studying business administration.

"I had a scholarship my first year at Tri-State University, which is now called Trine University, but the school was really known for its engineering program. After the first year I did not see the point of spending forty thousand dollars a year on a private university no one had heard of for a business degree."

While at school in Gola, he got his first taste of the hotel industry, working full-time for a Holiday Express hotel, starting as a front desk manager. He did not know at that time it would become his life's work.

"I worked there for about one year and then transferred with the company to Auburn, Indiana as an operations manager for two hotels. I started my second year of college in nearby Fort Wayne at a combined Indiana University and Purdue University campus. I majored in business administration at Indiana and public relations at Purdue and graduated with degrees from both schools."

Commuting to Auburn each day, though, took its toll and nineteen-year-old Tony soon found another full-time job in Fort Wayne as the general manager of another hotel, which provided him with additional training for certification as a hospitality administrator.

But his entrepreneurial instincts kicked in after a year managing the hotel. Tony purchased his first hotel property when he was just twenty, funded by the money he made from a new venture as a real estate broker.

"While at the hotel, I dated a guy who was a realtor and he convinced me to get my real estate license. I did and ended up selling five homes. I quit my hotel job because I was working less and making more money in real estate, which was important since I was taking a full sixteen units a semester at school. I used that money to help buy and renovate an old abandoned mansion in the historic district of Fort Wayne. I turned it into a very profitable luxury bed and breakfast."

Tony missed a lot of classes during the year it took to renovate and open his B&B, so it took him five years to graduate with his two bachelor degrees. But even before graduation he was on, again, to something new.

"I operated the B&B for about a year and then I flipped it and got a job with the Fort Wayne Philharmonic Orchestra as their sales manager. I kept that job until I graduated in 2008, just in time for the global recession. Job prospects were not great at home, so I decided it was a good time to move to Mexico and get my MBA."

He researched schools in Mexico and found a university in Puebla that had the graduate program and accreditation he was looking for. Satisfied that he had chosen the right school, Tony packed his bags and headed south. After the summer session he learned that the student loan he had applied for was no longer available, but he went ahead and enrolled for fall.

"I was kicked out of school after the fall semester for not paying, so I moved to a shared apartment with a few other guys in Playa del Carmen, a smaller beach resort just south of Cancun. I had been there before and really loved it."

Tony landed in Playa del Carmen without a plan, but confident in his ability to make things happen. He had a little bit of money left that he had made consulting with a B&B back home to take care of his immediate needs.

"I was twenty-three at the time and with school and jobs really had not had time to enjoy myself. For about a year I just bummed around at the beach and drank way too much."

But the entrepreneur in Tony would not let him rest for long. He started consulting again with a few small independent hotels in Playa del Carmen and a Holiday Inn Express to help them improve their revenue and profitability.

One of the hotels he handled had an enviable occupancy rate of about ninety percent, but was still not very profitable. After analyzing the hotel's business, Tony quickly determined that the occupancy rate was high because the hotel was selling rooms to tour operators for just forty-five dollars a night. He lowered the hotel's occupancy rate to sixty percent and increased revenue by thirty percent by establishing a better balance between occupancy and the rate charged. He also added new travel agencies to funnel tourists to the hotel based on the commissions they charged and what was needed to fill rooms profitably.

"I set up a system to include independent hotels in the global travel distribution system, which is used by all travel agencies in the world for booking reservations. Marriott, Hilton, Intercontinental and other big hotel chains are listed, but most independents are not. The system I developed connected small, independent hotels."

He signed up about thirty-five hotels in the area and was just getting off the ground with the program when the swine flu hit Mexico. Tony, and many others in the country, never believed it was a health crisis but rather a story blown out of proportion by the U.S. media. Regardless, it killed the tourism business in Playa del Carmen and Cancun. Tony invested the funds to get his system set up, but none of the hotels paid him and he was left with nothing.

Out of money, Tony had to regroup. He had a friend in South Carolina who had just closed a B&B he owned in Delaware. Tony persuaded him to reopen the bed and breakfast on the beach and let him run it, just for the summer. He made enough money to return to Mexico to start over in 2009 as a sales manager for several hotels in Playa del Carmen. But that did not last.

"I did a bit of everything for a year or so, but I learned the hard way that, in Mexico, things are not always what is promised. You sign up for a job and find out that it is not at all what you expected."

He was hired for an international sales manager job for a company that provided audio-visual equipment for big events at hotels in Cancun but soon discovered the company already had a sales manager. The local hotels required the company to have an English-speaking American on its payroll. He spent his days doing nothing but gazing at the beach.

He left that job quickly and took a job for a year as a dive master back in Playa del Carmen. His parents, both scuba diving instructors, came down and dove with him every day to help prepare him for his certification as a dive master.

Tony learned to speak fluent Spanish while living in Playa del Carmen. He had taken a Spanish immersion course when he first arrived in Puebla for college, but his fluency came through socializing in the evening with the local population of young Mexicans, who spoke English during the day to tourists and Spanish at night among themselves. Many in the local expat community, made up mostly of Europeans and South Americans and some Americans and Canadians, also spoke Spanish.

"Although I loved Playa del Carmen, I left when I was twenty-eight. By then I actually was one of the older people who lived there. It is a very young place with lots of people who are right out of college. I guess it is strange to say, but by then I was the old guy in Playa del Carmen."

Tony left his beach town in 2011 and moved to Mexico City, a sprawling megalopolis of nearly twenty-two million people and the largest city in the Americas. The capital of Mexico, the city sits over seven thousand feet high in the Valley of Mexico on the south end of Mexico's central plateau.

"I just wanted the city. I loved my time at the beach but it is hard to make friends. People come and go all the time in a resort town. I had a couple of hotels in Tulum and Playa del Carmen as sales and marketing clients but I found I could work from home and home could be Mexico

City. I absolutely love Mexico City. I think it is one of my absolute favorite places in the world. I could see myself living there for a long time."

He moved to a neighborhood adjacent to Chapultepec Park, rented an apartment and added a new hotel sales and marketing client in Mexico City. He had established a U.S.-based corporation called Namaste Hospitality in 2008 specifically to serve his growing hotel industry consulting business, which by now was flourishing.

Tony lived in Mexico City for about nine months. While there, by chance, he found a new opportunity that would lead to him to his dream of running his own hotel.

"I was visiting my mother in the states and a few of her friends asked what I was doing in Mexico. One of her friends said, 'We have a place in Chapala that we spent eight years renovating but have never lived there since renovating it two years ago. It would make a great hotel.'"

Two months later, Tony's mother rented the house for a week while he was attending a conference in Guadalajara. He made the forty-five-minute drive south to the small village of Ajijic on the northern shore of Lake Chapala, Mexico's largest natural lake, to see his mother and the property.

"It was a lot smaller than I had imagined. It was only four rooms, not large enough for a hotel, but perfect for a luxury B&B. I liked the idea of getting my hands on a hotel again as an owner, not just sales and marketing. I started talking with the owners seriously in 2012 and agreed to lease it. My idea was to expand into an empty lot next door to increase the size of the property, but the two brothers who owned the land were continually fighting over it so I eliminated that option."

Once the lease was signed in August of 2012, Tony had just two months to get the property ready for his first guests in October. He invested thirty thousand dollars of his own money to remodel the over seven thousand square foot former hacienda that sits several blocks up the hill from Lake Chapala and just a few blocks west of Ajijic's historic main plaza.

"It had not been lived in for two years and needed quite a bit of additional work. It was a beautiful old hacienda with a spacious tiled courtyard and pool surrounded by four separate apartments, a commercial-size kitchen and an enormous common living room. Besides basic electrical work and things like that, I bought new linens, some furniture, beds, art work and other amenities that brought it up to the standards of a luxury bed and breakfast."

Hacienda del Lago opened on time and quickly became the place to stay in Ajijic, which is renowned for its year-round, spring-like climate and one of the largest expat colonies in Mexico, many of them artists and writers.

With the success of Hacienda del Lago, Tony moved to a rental home in town but found he was uncomfortable living among the mostly American and Canadian expats of Ajijic.

"I did not move from Mexico City to live in the middle of a large expat community. I love the climate and I love the feeling of the town, but I am not the typical American expat. Most of my friends are Mexican and I speak Spanish all of the time."

Tony found that local expats live there because they either want a new life in Mexico or cannot afford to live in the U.S. But he is skeptical that Mexico is now that much cheaper than the United States.

"It is getting more and more expensive to live in Mexico. My mortgage in Indiana, for example, was just over four hundred dollars a month.

You cannot get a decent place to live here for that amount of money. For people coming from the Midwest and other lower cost of living areas in the U.S., it really is not that much cheaper. You have to spend at least six hundred to eight hundred dollars a month just to get a very modest two-bedroom apartment in a local neighborhood. On the other hand, if you are moving from California, it probably will seem like a bargain."

After two years of developing Hacienda del Lago into a successful luxury B&B, Tony was ready for his next adventure. That required turning over the property's day-to-day management to his business partner, Abraham. The two had met in Playa del Carmen when they were working on hotel projects together.

Now satisfied that operations were running smoothly in Ajijic under the management of Abraham, Tony turned his attention to a new business opportunity farther south. Much farther south.

Tony had a friend in Guadalajara who had worked in private equity placements for years before entering the U.S. Foreign Service in the her late forties. She told him that when she worked for a private equity firm, people sometimes came to her with projects in Argentina. The firm declined to invest because they did not believe Argentina was a great place for investment due to liquidity issues. Although her firm did not invest, she saw opportunity and personally invested in a winery in Argentina and some hotels. She recommended that Tony consider Argentina as a place to start a business.

Meanwhile, after investing so much time and energy in making Hacienda del Lago a success, Tony treated himself and a friend to a vacation in New York City. While there, they reconnected with an old friend from Argentina who also told Tony that Argentina had many opportunities for young entrepreneurs.

Back home, the itch to try something new and move on began again.

"I was in my hotel room late one night talking to my friend in Buenos Aires on Skype and he convinced me to fly down to see if I could find any opportunities that might make sense for me."

Tony packed two large suitcases and flew to Buenos Aires the following week for a month.

"I loved it. I had most of my things with me and thought if I really love it, I will just leave things here, and that is what I did. I rented a place in Via Crespo close to downtown, bought a car and started settling in."

Tony quickly recognized that the economic conditions in Argentina were favorable for a new business. The economy seemed to have bottomed out and since tourism is a dollar-and-Euro-driven business worldwide, the exchange rate was very favorable. Most importantly, he saw an opportunity to bring hotel sales outsourcing to independent hotels in Buenos Aires.

"Most of the hotels were poorly run because they were family owned or they just did not know anything about how hotels really work. Many did not even have reservations on their own website and did not sell through travel agencies."

Because of local laws, Tony was required to form a legal business entity in Argentina. His new company in Buenos Aires takes over the sales operation for each hotel they contract with for a percentage of hotel sales. They provide the hotels with a local telephone number for each country and then provide sales people to answer each call. For example, in the U.S., each Buenos Aires hotel that his company works with has a U.S. 800-number. Each call through the 800- number is answered and handled by Tony's sales staff.

"My sales staff works directly for me. They are responsible for managing each account to build the hotel's business. Getting a good sales person is very expensive because it is not like selling anything else. You have to have contacts with big travel agencies and websites, like tripadvisor.com, expedia.com and the other big online travel sites. They have to really know how contracting and packaging works and be able to do that for their clients. Independent hotels do not have that expertise."

The company also has outside sales people in Buenos Aires who find independent hotel clients and become the day-to-day face of the business. They are paid a combination of salary and commission. But all travel agency contracting, revenue management, reservations and other similar tasks remain with Tony's office sales staff.

Although the business in Argentina primarily is set up for sales outsourcing, Tony also helps some individual hotels launch, rebrand or restructure their properties for a fee.

"Right now the money potential I see is Argentina, but the world economy and regulations often change quickly. When the opportunity dries up here I will move on. I am always completely open to new adventures."

Tony also is intent on further developing the consulting side of his business to help fund investments in other ownership opportunities.

"Another side of the company I am working on is pairing investors for hotel investment projects. The problem with most smaller hotels that have twenty or thirty rooms is the investment is not big enough for a big investor, but too big for a smaller investor. I would like to put together an investment co-op to fund the purchase of smaller hotels. We could put together a nice package that would help provide financing and also help hotels shape up their bottom lines by improving their overall operations and sales."

Will Tony eventually get his fill of being an expat entrepreneur? It is doubtful. There are not many places he enjoys in the United States and he believes that most Americans are overwhelmingly negative.

"The minute you land in the United States you can see it. There is a prevailing ignorance and pride in that ignorance that I just find embarrassing. One of the real blessings of being an expat is that it gives you a whole different perspective on your home country, something I hear constantly from many other expats."

Tony will continue to live in Buenos Aires as long as his business does well, and tend to his investment in Hacienda del Lago in Ajijic. But his plans also include traveling the world to New York, Paris and other favorite cities.

"I'll remain in Latin America because I like it here, I speak the language and I can live well. Also, Mexico City and Buenos Aires are very large, cosmopolitan international cities that I love and they both have lots of things to offer me. But very importantly, the cost of living is wonderful. I can get a bottle of champagne for seven dollars in Buenos Aires. You just cannot beat that."

CHAPTER 3

Amanda Mouttaki
Age 30
Marrakesh, Morocco

"I grew up in the upper peninsula of Michigan in a very small rural community. There were two kinds of people that grew up there: people who loved it and knew they were going to stay there the rest of their lives, and people who were waiting and counting down the days until they could leave and never come back. I never came back."

AMANDA WAS ALWAYS interested in travel, geography, people and different cultures. When she was just sixteen she traveled to Athens, the Greek islands and Ephesus on Turkey's emerald coast on a school-sponsored trip. When she arrived in Athens she knew that traveling and living internationally would be an important part of her life.

She had no idea then how important it would be.

"When I was nineteen my father said he wanted to take my sixteen-year-old sister and me on a trip with him. Not just the usual trip to Florida, but anywhere in the world. The caveat was we had to agree on the destination and plan the trip together. The decision was Morocco and it changed my life forever."

During the second week of their trip, while visiting Marrakesh, her free-spirited younger sister invited a boy to visit them at the place they were staying. He brought along a friend who later became Amanda's husband.

"I was not interested at first but when I slowly turned and saw him I thought to myself, 'This is the guy I am going to marry.'"

His name was Youssef and he was just a year older than Amanda. They carried on their first conversation in French because Amanda knew no Arabic and Youssef knew no English, but they did know something special was happening between them.

They exchanged email addresses and began writing each other every day. Amanda, who had started college at Michigan State University, was now a sophomore at the Eau Claire branch of the University of Wisconsin, studying international political science.

"Not long after I returned Youssef asked me if I would come back to Marrakesh and spend some time so we could get to know each other, which made me very happy. During spring break I found a low airfare and hopped a plane to Morocco. Thankfully, my parents did not object because they always knew I was a really free spirit and had always trusted me."

The first day she arrived in Marrakesh, Youssef proposed to her. "Looking back, I think, what the heck was I doing, but I knew it was right. I think I knew it from the first time we met."

Amanda returned to school in Eau Claire and applied for a visa to bring Youssef to the United States. It was not easy getting a visa in 2004, just a few years after the catastrophic events of September 11, 2001. There were few tourist visas being issued to men of his age from that part of the world.

Amanda returned again to Marrakesh during the summer of 2004 for nearly two months to really get to know Youssef and his family. By December, her future husband had his visa interview and the next day was given a K-1 visa, known as a fiancée visa.

"I was in my last semester of school when Youssef arrived in Minneapolis in January of 2005. It was so funny because he had never seen snow before and there was plenty to see on the drive from the airport to Eau Claire. We got married three months later in April just before I graduated."

After graduation they decided to move to Washington D.C. because the capital had a large Moroccan community, which helped make Youssef more comfortable, particularly with his limited English. Amanda found a job working for the Islamic Society of North America on Capitol Hill and then left for a human resources recruiting position for a government contractor. But after three years, they returned to Eau Claire, mainly because of D.C.'s cost of living and poor school system.

Amanda had started an MBA program with Strayer University, an on-line school, while living in D.C. and finished her last semester back home in Eau Claire. They lived with her parents until she could find a job, which took nearly a year. Meanwhile, Youssef enrolled in a computer programming school to lay a foundation for his future employment in the information technology industry.

She eventually found work with a non-profit organization in the area, doing similar work to what she had done with the Islamic Society of North America: community outreach, project management and social media and blogging.

Amanda had started a blog and a website when they first moved to D.C., but that was mostly for fun. Back in Eau Claire she began to realize that she could actually make money from this line of business. She started earning an income from her online business through paid posts and product reviews. Most importantly, it seeded the idea of having a business that would make them location independent.

"When I became self-employed we realized there was a way we could move to Morocco without needing a contract for work or working for someone. We really wanted to move because it was very important to me that my children have a relationship with my husband's family."

The couple began seriously discussing a move to Marrakesh in 2012 after Youssef received full U.S. citizenship, which allowed him to remain outside of the United States for any length of time.

"There came a point several years ago where we said we cannot keep waiting. Our oldest son was eight at the time and I felt that if we waited any longer, it would be much more difficult for him to make the transition to a completely new environment."

After sitting down and looking at their budget, the couple decided to make their move to Morocco in August of 2013, but with a caveat. They gave themselves one year to make things work for them and their two boys, Mikhail and Khalil.

"Since we had decided to go for a year, we did not sell everything. We put lots of things in storage in Eau Claire and shipped the rest using an international moving company. It is not like moving to Texas, for sure. There are so many things to consider, like establishing power of attorney for someone to look after our bank account. Luckily, my experience as a project manager came in very handy. I made a list of everything I could think of and then picked three tasks everyday to accomplish. It worked."

They shipped a number of boxes to Morocco, which took about seven weeks. Rather than sending them straight through to Marrakesh, they drove to the port city of Casablanca, over one hundred miles away, to pick up their goods, worried that things might go missing enroute between the port of entry and their new home.

"If I had it to do over again, I would not have bothered shipping our goods by boat. I would have added six more suitcases. When we arrived we had virtually nothing for almost two months."

They moved into Youssef's family home, a multi-storied riad, a traditional Moroccan house with an interior garden or courtyard. The word riad comes from the Arabian term for garden.

"The riad we live in has three floors plus a roof floor, which is typically used by servants. We live on the third floor, which is basically an apartment with two bedrooms, a living room, a kitchen and a bathroom. My mother-in-law and sister-in-law live on the first and second floors. Because of the spacious interior garden we can easily lean over the railing and have a chat with them, but the open architecture also can make it a bit noisy."

After moving in, the first order of business for the family was to find a school for nine-year-old Mikhail and seven-year-old Khalil.

"We would have liked to have found a good school before we moved, but we could not really do anything before we physically moved here. Everything in Morocco is done face-to-face and you have to go to the education ministry for everything, which is a lot of bureaucracy to deal with."

They did not consider Moroccan public schools because of the quality of education and Youssef's experience with the local system. They looked at American, French and Canadian international schools and even considered homeschooling, but finally decided they wanted a school where their kids could learn both French and Arabic.

They settled on a private Moroccan school not far from their home that offered a half day of instruction in Arabic and the other half in French, with about a half hour of English each week. The principal of the school was trained in England and speaks fluent English, a big help to Amanda, who spoke no Arabic and just a little French.

"In Morocco, it is not even a question of having exposure to a second language. You are going to know two languages, and by the time you are finished with high school, maybe four or five. Our boys, for example, have two math books, a math book in Arabic and one in French."

The school's curriculum also is quite different from U.S. schools. While American schools focus more on independent, creative and critical thinking, the local curriculum places emphasis primarily on skills-based learning like reading and writing.

Culture also plays a strong role in schooling. "We do not believe in physical punishment for our children, but there is still a culture of physical punishment in Morocco. It is not really legal but it still happens. We were really firm with the school administration and teachers from the beginning. We told them we did not want them to touch our children in any disciplinary way."

Amanda initially felt a loss of independence in Morocco, not because of Moroccan society and culture, but because of language.

"I could still go do things for the first year or so but I was afraid that someone was going to talk to me and I would not be able to respond.

There were times when I thought I should go back home where everything made sense. The hardest thing was the loss of independence. I could not even go to the bakery to pick up a loaf of bread because I did not know what to say."

Both her Arabic and French language skills have improved and she feels somewhat more independent now, but a feeling of not fitting in still remains.

"I was talking to an expat friend of mine about not fitting in anywhere. You no longer fit in the country you were born in because you have this other experience and dimension to your life that most people there do not have. But you also do not really fit in your new country because you are always going to be a foreigner."

A wide range of expats populate Marrakesh and the rest of Morocco, from the very wealthy, to those who moved for religious purposes, to free-spirited single expats looking for an adventure. Most are British and French, but some are American.

"I am an American married to a Moroccan living in a very residential part of the city leading the regular day-to-day life of a Moroccan. Yet few of my friends are Moroccan, partly because my language skills are still not adequate. A neighbor, for example, invited my boys over for her daughter's birthday party. If I spoke Arabic fluently I can see where she and I might become good friends, but I am at a point where that cannot happen yet. Most of my friends are American or expats from other countries that speak English."

Even with the frustration she feels when she cannot communicate well, Amanda is very happy with her life. She has not encountered a level of frustration that would make her want to go home, as some expats experience.

Robert Nelson

"I like my day-to-day life. I like living here for all the frustrations. My life is much less stressful and you cannot buy that. I am able to have help with my kids because my husband has a very large family and we also get to travel a lot, particularly to other Mediterranean countries. Living here has also allowed me to do what I have always wanted to do: travel, write and share my experiences with other people."

Some of those experiences are good and some not so good. Marrakesh is the fourth largest city in Morocco with a population of nearly one million people, but it swells several million more each year with the arrival of tourists from all over the world.

"Tourism is the bread and butter for local people, but I am not a fan of all the tourists who visit. For some reason, maybe because Marrakesh is considered to be somewhat exotic, tourists forget their manners when they come here. They think nothing of putting a camera in your face and taking a picture. Many people here do not like having their picture taken for this reason. This is not a zoo."

Though they are living nearly five thousand miles from family and friends, the mystique of Marrakesh has drawn many to visit them. "I have seen more friends and family in the last year and a half than when we lived close to them in the U.S."

Amanda stays in touch daily with her family and friends via the Internet, a miracle of modern communication technology. She returned home for two months during the summer of 2014 to see everyone and saw a big difference between her two boys and the kids she knows back home.

"First, our kids have the ability now to speak three languages fluently, Arabic, French and English. Because of these language abilities, they will have amazing job opportunities when they grow up. And, because of our location, we can take them anywhere in Europe, Africa and the Middle

East relatively quickly and inexpensively. How many kids do you know who go to Scotland on their school break?"

Amanda has settled in well and is using the skills and knowledge gained from operating her own blog and website in the U.S. and working remotely for several companies.

"I hated working for companies when I was gone from seven in the morning until seven in the evening every day. Right before I left the U.S. I was working for a public relations firm as a contractor and then as an employee. I was able to work from home and enjoy the flexibility that comes from a job that can be done online. It was really that experience that led me to see that I could make a full-time living not ever going into an office."

When they made the decision to move, the public relations company said she could continue working remotely, but it still was not enough to live on.

"I had been writing for a Moroccan travel company while in Wisconsin, but they restructured and eliminated the job. I let them know I was moving to Morocco and they offered me a new position as blog editor and social media coordinator."

The two jobs were still not enough, though, so Amanda expanded her freelance writing and continued developing her own blog, marocmama.com, which provides her view of life in Morocco, travel and food tips from around the world, resources and other information.

As business improved, Amanda was able to stop working for the public relations firm and focus more on her blog and freelance writing and a new business she and Youssef had started, called Marrakesh Food Tours.

"The first time I came to Morocco when I was nineteen I hated the food. We ate the same tourist food every single day. But when I returned to spend time with Youssef and his family, I discovered how wonderful Moroccan food is. I can now cook most Moroccan food."

This experience was inspiration for the Mouttaki's new business. "I just kept thinking 'Oh my gosh, tourists are going to leave here and have the same opinion of Moroccan food as I did,' so I did some research to see what existed in Marrakesh because I knew food tours were very popular around the world. I thought there must be something here already, but there was not."

She built a website for the new business and began writing about what to eat and what to avoid in Marrakesh on her blog. She promoted the new business and offered a link to the Marrakesh Food Tours website and had four reservations within the first 36 hours.

"I love living here and wanted people to walk away and feel like they had at least one positive experience in Marrakesh. The walking tour lasts about three hours, depending on how many people are in the group. We only do a maximum of six people in each group."

They offer two tours, the first at one in the afternoon and the evening tour at six p.m. The itinerary includes small family run restaurants where grandma cooks the food, to street stalls. The evening tour generally features more traditional Moroccan food, but they also offer what they call "freaky foods," which may include things like snail soup and spleen loaf. Her guideline is: "Would my mother-in-law eat it?"

The tour costs sixty dollars per person, but private tours are also offered for a higher price. "We had a group of chefs from England that wanted a special tour, so they paid a different rate."

Starting their business was not a piece of cake because in Morocco, you must hire an accountant to handle all the licenses and paperwork for you. They found a good one through a friend of theirs. "As the saying goes, 'The French left in the nineteen-sixties, but none of the paperwork ever changed.' We just paid a flat fee to get all the necessary documents done. There is no way we could have done this by ourselves."

The business is flourishing now, partly due to Youssef's local connections. "He knew the right people and Morocco is very much a network society. You really need to know the right people to get things done."

Amanda and her family love their life in Morocco but they are also looking ahead to the future, which probably does not include another ex-pat experience in a different country.

"We take it one year at a time but I do not see us living here longer than three more years. Once our oldest son reaches high school age, we will quite likely return to the U.S. so both kids can go to an American high school, which we think is best to prepare them for college. By then they will have a strong foundation in French and Arabic and a cultural experience they will never forget. Most importantly, they will truly know Youssef's family."

They would like to keep their options open, though. "Maybe we will come back when the boys leave home or perhaps spend part of the year here. The nice thing about the type of lifestyle we have in Marrakesh is that you can live comfortably without being wealthy."

CHAPTER 4

—— ✖ ——

Heather Etchevers
Age 44
Marseilles, France

"I immigrated to France in the early nineteen-nineties. If you think about it, in America we would not think twice about somebody who immigrated from Cambodia or Korea or France to set up a business or work as a scientist for the National Institutes of Health. It is a very normal experience. But an American doing that, in the other direction, it is a little strange."

HEATHER'S JOURNEY TO Marseilles began in the Boston area, Newton to be specific.

Dad was an electrical engineer and mom, a former English teacher, stayed at home to raise Heather and her younger brother.

As a child Heather was drawn to languages, French in particular. Her mother arranged private lessons for her in the fifth grade and she continued studying the language through high school.

"By the time I got to junior high school I was really gung-ho for taking French. In the Boston area we have a lot of ties to the people in New England who are of French-Canadian extraction. I made some good friends who also were really drawn to the language. I found it easy and fun."

Adventurers Abroad

After high school, Heather remained close to home and attended Wellesley College, a private women's liberal-arts college in Wellesley, Massachusetts. She majored in biology, minored in music and played the clarinet. While there, she spent her junior year at Oxford University to get a taste of living abroad. Back home, her senior year proved to be life changing for her.

"I was the resident advisor for my dorm that year and invited a young woman on my floor to a party a friend of mine was having in another dorm to cheer her up.

I met a young man from France at the party who was studying in a master's program at the Massachusetts Institute of Technology. His name was Olivier and a few years later, he would become my husband."

After graduation, Heather spent the summer in Germany attending a music program, the *Internationale Ferienkurse für Neue Musik* in Darmstadt, and then headed west to enroll in the doctoral program at the University of California – Berkeley.

Olivier had graduated from MIT and returned to his home in Paris. But Heather was on his mind, so he came to visit her in Berkeley that fall. The romance began to bloom and after a year and a half, Heather knew that Olivier really mattered to her.

"After a while at Berkeley I was able to arrange a lab internship in Paris for a semester so Olivier and I could get to know each other better. We lived together in an apartment in the fifteenth arrondissement."

Heather returned to Berkeley after the internship and soon passed her qualifying exams for her Ph.D. She returned to Paris and Olivier in 1994 to finish her Ph.D. program in molecular and cell biology. They were married in a French civil ceremony in 1995, followed a few months later by a more formal wedding in the U.S. To ensure that someone would give her a diploma, Heather also decided to co-enroll in an equivalent degree program at the University of Paris' Pierre et Marie Curie campus. She was awarded her Ph.D. from U.C. Berkeley in 1998 and received the equivalency from the University of Paris six months later, after a public defense.

But the 1990s were not just the grind of academic life for Heather. She and Olivier welcomed their first child, a son named Emilien, in 1997.

"There were nine of us who were pregnant in the lab that year. Since I worked in embryology we liked to joke that it was really applied embryology and Emilien was the result."

Daughter Marjorie followed two years later, but a rare congenital condition caused worry for the family.

"When my daughter was born, I was still working in the same laboratory I had been working in while getting my doctorate. I was given a fellowship for post-doctoral work in the lab and wanted to continue in this environment because our daughter was born with a major malformation of her skin, an extremely large mole on her lower back known as the giant congenital melanocytic nevus. The work I was doing, and continue to this day, happened to be very relevant to her condition because it was focused on what a particular type of stem cell does in the developing embryo."

Marjorie underwent seven operations of reconstructive plastic surgery at the Necker Children's Hospital in Paris, most before preschool, until the malformation was nearly completely removed.

During this time, Heather began looking for opportunities where she could apply her knowledge of the molecular bases of birth defects. She found a genetics lab in Paris that was looking for someone with her background, and in 2001 began working at Necker Children's Hospital, which has been the premier children's hospital of continental Europe since just before the French Revolution.

"At that point, I think I truly diverged from the typical expat experience. I was aiming to integrate as a tenured researcher into the French research system. By the time my daughter was born, I had a fair amount of experience in the French workplace."

She received a tenured position in 2004 with France's National Institute for Health and Medical Research, or INSERM, strongly based on receiving a Futures (Avenir) Program award, one of the first awards of its kind given.

"This program was something new that the government set up to help young researchers. I was one of the first recipients and received a three-year startup package that funded my work. It led to being offered a tenured position."

However, the stress of being part of an urban, inter-cultural couple working full-time while caring for two young children - one with special needs - took its toll on Heather's health. She underwent a period of depression, which was exacerbated by the helplessness she shared with all expats after the terrorist attacks on the U.S. September 11, 2001. By November, Heather was hospitalized for a ruptured appendix, but after treatment and a full, if slow, recovery, things began to look up again for the family. Heather credits some of the benefits provided by the French government, like child and after-school day care, ample paid vacation and flex time at work, as well as cultural family solidarity, for keeping it together.

In 2006, Olivier, who had been working in procurement for the French Air Force, was offered a position in Toulouse, located over three hundred miles southwest of Paris. The city is the center of the European aerospace industry because of the historical presence of Airbus, the large airplane manufacturer headquartered in Toulouse. He became the program manager for procurement of a military transporter known as the A400M, on behalf of a European Union program, the Organisation for Joint Armament Cooperation (OCCAR).

"Toulouse was a place we were happy to live in. We rented out our smallish apartment in the Paris suburbs and rented a sixteen hundred square foot home in Toulouse for the same amount of money. It was a beautiful old farmhouse with a very large backyard and garden. I loved it because I could bike to work for the first time ever."

But relocating to Toulouse was not perfectly idyllic. Heather's mother in Newton died suddenly the week after they arrived, which was when French intergenerational family support came into play. Her in-laws came to Toulouse to manage the household and help the kids start school, so Heather could return to the U.S. for two weeks to assist her brother.

For the next three years the family lived in southwestern France, but Heather had to commute to Paris for an overnight every two weeks. She was able to stay with her in-laws, which helped make the time away from her family more comfortable and somewhat less stressful, although the arrangement required compromises on all sides.

"By then I had my first Ph.D. student and a second postdoc in Paris. I accepted an arrangement where I would work twenty percent of my time in Paris and eighty percent of my time in Toulouse. I worked with a laboratory in Toulouse that studies genetic causes of birth defects of the eye and then I would fly to Paris to try to run the lab there."

One of the benefits of their new location was its proximity to Olivier's family ancestral home in the Pyrenees Mountains, which separate France from Spain.

"We used it often when we were in Toulouse because it was just an hour and a half drive away. My mother-in-law's great-grandfather was a schoolteacher in this little village right in the middle of the Pyrenees, close to a national park. We would go there every summer and sometimes there would be four generations sharing the house at the same time. The family had been using the home for get-togethers during the summer since at least Olivier's grandmother's childhood. The home was built before the French Revolution. When we went in the nineteen-nineties it still did not have hot water, but we really did not mind. The toilet was indoors by that point, though there is still no central heat. It is quite wonderful. We even found books from the eighteenth century in the attic reused for notepaper by the schoolteacher."

Life changed for the family again in 2009 when Olivier's contract with OCCAR was over and he found a new job with Eurocopter, now called Airbus Helicopter, in Marseilles.

Meanwhile, Heather and the kids returned to their former apartment for a year, not sure whether or not to give up their support system in Paris for the uncertainty of Olivier's new job with a private firm. Heather began working full-time again in her INSERM group at the Necker Children's Hospital and the kids made the transition back to schools in their old neighborhood. Olivier commuted to Paris on weekends, and the family visited him in the south and house-hunted during school vacations.

"A real advantage working for national research organizations in France is that as a tenured scientist, you can take your position with you wherever you want to go, as long as you can make a rational case for joining another laboratory. The disadvantage is a much-reduced salary relative to what I could enjoy, if I had an equivalent position in an English-speaking country. It's exquisitely difficult for single parents."

Heather made a case to the INSERM for why she should transfer to a genetics unit carrying out research in Marseilles. They accepted her proposal, so the couple sold their Paris apartment, and she headed south with the kids to join Olivier in Marseilles in 2010.

They were able to purchase a house midway between Marseilles and Aix-en-Provence. Olivier's job at the time was close to Aix and Heather worked in the very heart of Marseilles, so they split the commuting difference.

Heather's four-bedroom home sits at the top of a hill surrounded by wild asparagus, pines and oaks in a small town to the south of Aix. They keep a chicken for eggs and an outdoor cat for cuddles. The town hall is within eyesight of the house.

"The location was most convenient for our kids, who were both enrolled in a junior high school in Aix and then attended a public high school with a bilingual program a couple miles away from our home. We wanted a place where they could be more independent and use the bus to get around. I also decided recently to use the bus for commuting after many frustrating hours behind the wheel trying to get to my job in downtown Marseilles."

Emilien, now eighteen, is in an advanced college prep track as preparation for the *grandes écoles* higher education system in France. The selective two-year program is somewhat like an associate or community college-level degree that is offered at only some high schools in France.

"It is really distinct to France and has no equivalency in America. It allows him to enter college as a junior or go to an elite engineering school, which is what he would prefer. With their schooling, we wanted to ensure that our children had as many options as possible that would allow them to choose their own way."

Heather was a tiny bit disappointed that Emilien was so set on staying within French higher education, but he is thriving. Marjorie, fifteen, is more interested in looking into what the U.S. and Canada, or perhaps England, might have to offer for a liberal arts college degree.

Life in the south of France is sweet for the family and for the many expats found in Provence, some of whom Heather has come to know. Since the publication of a series of books on Provence by British author Peter Mayle through the nineteen-nineties, expats have flocked to the area. She began to meet local Americans when she attended a Democrats Abroad meeting in Aix and, along with about thirty others, was asked to introduce herself and talk about what she did. There was not a single person, other than her, that either worked directly for a French company or the government. Most were writers, painters or retirees.

"All the years I was in Paris I took great pains to avoid American expats because I really wanted to integrate and I worked with people from many countries. I received my French citizenship early on and feel connected to France. I think I realized at nineteen, though, that I was already part of a worldwide community of people without a single homeland. Those are the expats I am drawn to. Many Americans I have met in France are transient and not so interested in being integrated culturally; they pass judgments as outsiders. I do not want to deny who I am, a true American, but I want that extra level of what it is to know something special about the country in which you are living. I accept my immigrant status, which is probably distinct from how most people consider the word expatriate. But I still use my U.S. passport and declare my federal taxes, though I grumble about the useless paperwork."

She had found her kind of expat earlier, when the family moved to Toulouse. Through the Wellesley alumnae club in France, she met a woman who had graduated five years before her, who became her good friend.

"Through Rebecca, I was then introduced to a private group of working women in Toulouse who are English-speaking expats. About two-thirds of them were Americans, like me, who had settled in France and had really integrated into the culture and society. Many were writers and consultants, or running small businesses. People came and left because some would move back to America, others to Shanghai and other places. That is when I got more connected with American expats. They were so interesting with many different stories to tell."

Life in France is not quite all *joie de vivre* for Heather, though. She has had many frustrating moments trying to understand and deal with French culture.

"In America, people overall tend to say yes much more often and may or may not admit it cannot be done after all. The French are really good at saying no and then maybe reconsidering it later. There is a little truth to the stereotype of nations being either optimistic or pessimistic. Where you really feel it here is in dealing with people in administration. Many view it as a chore to do what we would just consider their job, whereas, in the U.S., there is more often some personal engagement and a willingness to help out. In France, it is really rare that someone goes that extra mile to help you, unless they feel they already know you personally."

She also still cannot get over the French national predilection for cutting in line.

"In France, if you can cut in line, it is almost your moral duty to try. As an American it seems very unfair to me. It frustrates me to no end. Traffic is the same thing. In Marseille, it is accepted to pass on the right side of the road, regardless of the safety hazard it presents. That's a culture shock even to Parisians."

Characteristic national behavioral differences aside, Heather has had to deal with very little culture shock over the years and has integrated smoothly into the rhythm of French life.

"I was thrilled to discover that France is not a cliché. There is a huge amount of cultural diversity, backgrounds and histories. The French really know how to respect and care for their past, which I appreciate greatly."

Life in France has nearly always agreed with Heather. Her roots are deep and her career is prospering in Marseilles. She continues to lead the way in biomedical science research for the congenital melanocytic nevus, her daughter's birth defect. Heather currently chairs the international scientific advisory council of Naevus Global, a federation of national patient groups.

"I am happy with my life in France. When I moved to Marseilles, I picked up my clarinet again and joined a wind band of mostly French, with a few expats. I also recently joined a university symphony orchestra. Getting involved with local people and activities is what really makes life living abroad – perhaps anywhere – truly enriching."

CHAPTER 5

Matthew Hatfield
Age 27
Daigo, Japan

"I felt like I had been looking for a lot of things in the States that I just could not find. Everyone seemed to be on a different wavelength. When I came to Japan, I felt different. I got more confident in myself and felt great about things. I opened up to Japan and got a lot in return."

MATTHEW HATFIELD FELL in love with Japanese animation when he was a kid living in Elk Grove, California, just a little south of Sacramento. He thought Japanese technology, video games and culture were very cool. So cool that he decided to study the Japanese language and culture in high school, somehow knowing that one day he would live there.

He spent most of his life in Elk Grove, primarily with his mother, an executive with California's State Parks and Recreation Department. His parents divorced when he was very young and his father, an executive recruiter, moved away and eventually remarried.

Growing up in Elk Grove, Matthew and his younger sister spent much of their leisure time watching movies, which later would prove beneficial to both. His sister, Caitlin, would become a budding actress and Matthew would discover a latent talent all good teachers must have: acting. He would put it to good use Japan.

After high school graduation, Matthew enrolled at the University of California, Davis, just over thirty miles away from his hometown.

"I started out as a philosophy major but I soon discovered that Davis was a really tough school. To make it through with decent grades, I decided to change my major to something I was good at and liked. Math, drafting and architectural stuff were things I liked and could do well in, so I switched to a visual communications major and graduated in 2010 with a bachelor's degree.

Like so many other Millennials, Matthew graduated into a very difficult job market, especially in California where unemployment was at an all-time high. Not able to find a good full-time job, he settled for a series of low-level jobs that would pay his rent and buy him time until the job market recovered.

"I was living with my girlfriend at that time and working a series of really crappy jobs. When we broke up, I lost my job and moved back home to live with my mom and take some time to figure out what I should do with my life. I started by going to the gym everyday to get healthy and then began looking for internships that would give me the experience to land a decent job."

While searching for an internship, Matthew connected with an old friend who had worked as an English teacher in Japan. He told Matthew that the company he had worked for, Interac, was the largest private provider of professional foreign teachers to the Japanese government and were hiring Americans to teach English there.

"As soon as he described the opportunity, I knew that it was time for me to break the cycle I was in. I had taken four years of Japanese, knew a bit about the culture and had always wanted to go there, so why not try it."

Matthew spent the next few months researching Interac, completing online application forms and questionnaires and interviewing with Interac recruiters.

"Interac was very thorough in vetting potential employees. When you do your interview with them, you have to do a demonstration lesson, which is taped and not easy if you have not done one before. They also ask you where you would like to be placed, since they have locations all around Japan."

Interact, which provides English teachers primarily for elementary and middle school grades in Japan, also required candidates to have a four-year college degree and some teaching experience. Matthew had a little experience teaching screen-printing while at UC Davis and some familiarity with the Japanese language and culture.

"I guess I did well in the interviews because Interact hired me and then gave me an orientation on Japan and what to expect. Things got a little hectic after I accepted their offer. The first thing I did was sell absolutely everything I had. The company told me that I would need about five thousand dollars to cover my airfare to Japan, first month's rent, a rental car and a few things like that. I got about ten thousand dollars from selling all of my stuff so I was set."

Before he left for his Japan adventure, Matthew spent hours on YouTube and other informational websites learning all he could about living and working in Japan.

"I think the most useful site I found was GaijinPot, a website all about Japan. I used the forum on the site a lot because it is used mainly by people living in Japan and I found that I could post my questions and get reliable answers. One of the biggest problems I ran into on the Internet is misinformation."

Adventurers Abroad

After packing some clothes and his toothbrush in a few bags, Matthew flew to Tokyo in late March of 2014 to first spend a week at a hotel with other new Interac English teachers learning the ropes. The new recruits were taught how to prepare a lesson plan, the curriculum they would be working with, Japanese culture and other information to equip them for success in their new jobs. The company also took care of finding him an apartment in his new town, getting him a work permit visa and all of the other necessary paperwork to live and work in Japan.

Although Matthew had to pay some of the initial bills when he arrived in Japan, his company paid for half of the rent on his car and a few other expenses. His contract with Interac is for one year and at the end of his year of employment, the company will decide if they want to keep him. Most people hired by Interac usually stay in Japan for two or three years.

"I live in Daigo, which is small town of about twenty thousand people about a three-hour drive northeast of Tokyo. I specifically requested a more rural assignment because I wanted to stay away from the high-prices and congestion of Tokyo. Daigo, though, is very close to a much larger city, Mito, which has a population of nearly three hundred thousand. I go there often."

Before Matthew arrived, his company had already found him a nice one-bedroom apartment with a small kitchen, bath and main living and sleeping room.

"Everything in my apartment is pretty much squashed together, which is very typical here. It is very difficult to find a large apartment in Japan. Many foreigners end up in what they call 'Leopalaces,' which are very tiny but functional apartments in giant apartment complexes. Since I live in a small town, I was more fortunate. My apartment is like a studio apartment in a little six-apartment building about a twenty-minute drive from where I work."

Whether just driving to work every day or to Tokyo or other places during the weekend, driving in Japan has been a challenge for Matthew. In Japan, traffic moves on the left, not on the right, completely opposite to what he was accustomed to in the U.S.

"It was terrifying at first but then I steadily got used to it the more I drove. The hardest thing to get used to was not driving on the 'wrong side of the road.' It actually was the size of my car. I am a lanky six-foot American and my rental car is this little black box with a 'bunny ears' emblem. It may be a cute little car but it is still a clown car."

Having a car makes Matthew's life much easier in Daigo. His job takes him to several locations throughout the town each week since he works at six different elementary and middle schools. He spends most of his time, though, at Namase Junior High School.

"I work at Namase about three and a half days a week and then rotate through the other schools. At Namase I co-teach with a Japanese teacher who speaks English. The majority of the time I am helping her and ensuring that words are pronounced correctly. At the elementary schools, I have forty-five minutes to teach a whole lesson by myself. The teacher is usually off to the side and helps only after I have finished. I did not realize that watching all of those movies as a kid could help me later in life. I have learned how to act things out. You know, gesturing is still a very universal language."

Matthew discovered that he enjoyed being a character in front of the kids. It was a revelation because he had felt so awkward back home. This was different for him. He now was vocal, funny and had their full attention. He was very nervous with his kids at first but once he started to get positive feedback from them, like laughing at his antics, he relaxed and started having fun. He also slowed down his speech so the students could better understand his English.

"I speak mostly English in class but when I do speak Japanese, I use the katakana form of Japanese, which is where you find foreign words that have come into the lexicon. It basically is what words would sound like if a Japanese person had said them. It is very easy to pronounce and talk with the students and say keywords in that tone so they can easily understand you. Katakana is different from the hiragana form of Japanese, which is the basic language of Japan."

When he is not teaching, Matthew likes to hop in his tiny car and visit friends. At first, his weekend destination was usually Tokyo, where friends from his initial training in Japan lived. But he soon found that his money did not go far in one of the most expensive cities in the world. A little lighter in his wallet, he decided to spend more time with new friends in his area of Japan.

"Since I have a car it is very easy to get around, which makes weekends a lot more fun. Most of the roads around Daigo are two-lane and in good shape, which is fine for my baby car. I like to drive through the green, wooded hills around Daigo and Mito, which are very beautiful. There also is a giant river, the Kuji River, that runs through town, which I cross every day on the way to work."

Matthew likes the rural setting of his small town and its proximity to many beautiful parks, such as the Kairaku-en in Mito, one of the three great gardens of Japan, known for its magnificent display of cherry blossoms in the spring. He also enjoys visiting an ancient Edo-period home on the very top of the mountain above the park. The home overlooks lovely Senba Lake in Kairaku-en where fireworks displays are often held.

"I think my happiest discovery about living here was that I did not miss the excitement of city life at all. I like all of this nature around me. I can relax and be alone here or do simple things with friends like visiting national parks or just driving through the countryside."

But day-to-day living in a small town is not without its challenges. Until recently, shopping in Daigo had been difficult for Matthew, especially food shopping. He was fortunate to have a small market across from his apartment that was a convenient location to pick up day-to-day necessities, but it really was not sufficient.

"It was right across the street and reminded me of some of the 'hole-in-the-wall' markets back home. Not much choice at all. But a new giant Safeway-like supermarket opened in town and that has really changed things for the better. It is probably the biggest thing to happen to Daigo in quite a long time."

Even with the arrival of the larger supermarket, Matthew still must travel to Mito, about an hour a way by car, for some of his needs.

"I can get most of what I need here, especially great food. I love Japanese food. It is really healthy and delicious. They find natural ways of simplifying the food, which brings out the flavors. I am usually not a big fan of vegetables, but they put a very light sauce on them here and all of a sudden it is the most amazing thing that I have every eaten. My taste buds still are not used to such great food. I grew up on crappy fast-food restaurants in California."

Language is still a problem for Matthew even though he studied Japanese in high school and loved it. He found it difficult at first to remember much of what he had learned and, although, English is taught from kindergarten through university in Japan, few in his area are truly fluent.

"Many will not speak English but they have an understanding of it, so that helps. Unfortunately, I lost most of my ability to speak Japanese because I had no real- world day-to-day application of it back in California. When I got to Daigo, I found a class run by older women who had volunteered to teach the language to the newest teacher working in the school system. Once I started with them, my Japanese language skills skyrocketed after about a month. I started picking things up very quickly and my brain started to feel comfortable with accepting it."

Matthew's goal is to pass the N1-level of the Japanese Learning Proficiency Test, the highest of five levels. Besides taking local language lessons, he also purchased a Japanese language application for his smartphone and an instruction book.

Most of his friends in Japan speak limited Japanese, also. They are mainly English-speaking expats he works with, either locally or those he met during his initial training in Tokyo who teach in other areas of the country.

"Our Interac training class in Tokyo was very small. We had about fifteen people. I was a very shy person back in California but I was resolved to break out of my shell in Japan. I just told myself that I am going to get to know everybody, and I did. When you are stuck in the same room for seventy-two hours, you get comfortable very quickly. I bonded with many of them during training and they have become friends."

Matthew also became friends with a New Zealand couple in Daigo who had started teaching at the same time he did, and a Jamaican woman who had been teaching there for nearly three years. A new friendship also is developing with a fellow Japanese teacher who also enjoys Matthew's passion for video games. They spend much of their time together hanging out in the nearby larger city of Mito on weekends.

As with many expats, Matthew uses social media to stay in touch with friends and family. He is still a big fan and user of GaijinPot, but also frequents Facebook groups, including Interac's Facebook page, which attracts fellow American English teachers for all over the world.

"Everyone I have met online seems very cool, no elitism or anything like that. Social media is a great way to learn new things about Japan, meet other expats and stay connected with them."

Matthew has integrated rather quickly into daily Japanese life in Daigo, partly a by-product of his Japanese language and culture study in high school and his love of the country that drove him to learn as much about Japan as he could before he left California.

"I think the biggest thing I had to get used to, and was not quite prepared for, was the homogeneity of the Japanese people. You will not find a lot of demographic variation in Japan because about ninety-eight percent are native Japanese. Americans, or foreigners in general, tend to stand out in Japan. I felt at first like I was in the spotlight all of the time. I was not quite prepared for that feeling."

But Matthew has adjusted and now feels quite at home. He believes he made a good choice when he decided to move to Japan and thinks many other Americans might find living the expat life to their liking.

"Moving to Japan or another country is ultimately a very personal decision, but I guarantee that someone who wants to be an expat will have their views of the world changed drastically. Their experience will be so much different from where they came from. But it really depends on the person. If they want to take a lot of chances, have an adventure and sell everything off and move, I think that is cool. They should just do it."

Matthew has no regrets about his move to Japan, particularly since his life at the time he moved had been stuck in low gear.

"For me, leaving the U.S. was good because I needed to break out the rut I was in. But I think, also, that it has been a little crazy in the U.S. lately. It all started with the crash of the economy but other things, like the shootings of unarmed black people and other craziness happening there, had me really thinking about living somewhere else. Now I see things from a completely different perspective, more of a world perspective and I think that is good."

Matthew's world perspective may change somewhat in the future as he contemplates the second act of his expat life in Morocco.

"When I finally moved here, I discovered how much I enjoy just experiencing new things. Japan today, the world tomorrow. I would like to just keep hopping around trying different places. My best friend from back home, who is living in the Netherlands with his girlfriend, is studying for his Teaching English as a Foreign Language (TEFL) certification. He has inspired me to do the same, and with my teaching experience in Japan, it should not be a problem. Once I get my certification, I plan to go to Morocco and teach there."

CHAPTER 6

Cordelia Rojas
Age 41
Bangkok, Thailand

"I have two young girls that I am trying to raise into global citizens, that is my dream. I want them to speak multiple languages. I want them to understand the world and the history of the world. I do not want them living back in the States, in that environment. We are not going back there any time soon."

CORDELIA ROJAS IS an independent, adventurous New York City woman who knows what she wants and is not afraid to do what it takes to get it. She learned from an early age to follow the road less traveled, which led her first to London and later to Singapore and Bangkok.

Cordelia's love of travel and adventure grew from the many vacation trips her family took. Her father, a New York City travel agent, gave Cordelia her first taste of travel, taking the family to new and exciting places almost every year. Her French mother also took Cordelia and her two brothers on long, carefree summers in the Loire Valley to see her family.

Her restless mind and high spirit created problems for Cordelia when she reached high school. She was easily bored and changed private schools every year until she finally moved out of her home at seventeen to live on her own.

She realized, though, that success in life would require a college degree. She took and passed the GED test for a high school equivalency diploma and enrolled at Hunter College in New York. To support herself, she worked at a series of retail jobs that helped her pay the bills.

"The original plan for my education was to move to California, establish residency there and then attend one of the state universities because tuition and fees were so much cheaper. But instead, I ended up going to my uncle's wedding in Europe and met a very charming Danish photographer. That was it. I moved to London for love when I was just twenty years old."

Cordelia did not like London at first but as she got to know the city and developed friendships, her opinion changed completely. She passed through a number of jobs in London, from an accountant's assistant to manager of a small Japanese print gallery, until an adventure in Turkey beckoned in 1999.

"I had always been interested in sailing and decided to learn how to sail when I lived in London. That led to a wonderful opportunity to teach sailing in Turkey. I really loved that job. I lived most of the time on the Datça Peninsula, which is located between the cities of Marmaris and Bodrum on Turkey's southwest coast. The travel brochures call it the turquoise coast because the water has that beautiful blue-green look. I felt like I could have lived there forever."

But she did not. After about a year, London came calling once again. This time, though, she found a job that excited her.

"I was very fortunate to work for the Work Foundation. I started as a temp but worked my way up to advisor to the chief executive officer. I helped the CEO manage his staff, prepare his speeches and plan his engagements, among other things. The organization was involved in all aspects of work, from discrimination at work to creativity at work. It was really a great job and I learned so much."

She also began to realize that further advancement at work would require a college degree, so she enrolled at Birkbeck, a research-oriented campus of the University of London, to study environmental science. She had become interested in the field when she observed how humans were polluting the Mediterranean Sea while teaching sailing in Turkey.

By now, Cordelia's life in London was very good and getting even better with her new job. But then love struck. Hard.

"I met my husband, Javier, online and fell madly in love with him. He was born and raised in Mexico but was working in New York City as an architect. It was the second time I crossed the Atlantic for love. I moved back to New York City in 2003 to be with him and finish my degree where I started many years ago, Hunter College."

When she first arrived, Cordelia found a job working on Wall Street for a financial firm but soon moved on to the research department of an advertising agency. After several tries, she finally found a job she liked, working for the executive director of PopTech, a non-profit organization that brings innovators from a variety of fields together to find solutions to the world's problems. This time she stayed for six years.

"That was an incredible job. I ended up managing the research on a number of collaboration projects. We were developing prototypes to test, like solar powered-fabrics. We had a conference every year and I got to meet a broad range of very fascinating people, including Richard Dawkins, the evolutionary biologist from Oxford University in England and *New York Times* columnist and author Thomas Friedman."

While working at PopTech, she finally graduated from college. After fifteen years, Hunter College awarded her a bachelor's degree in environmental studies. Now, with a great job and her education completed, Cordelia and Javier married in 2007. Life was going very well indeed for the couple. Almost too well.

"When the 2008 recession struck, New York City was hit very hard. Architecture firms usually suffer quickly in a major downturn when building projects dry up, but Javier was able to hang on for about a year before he lost his job."

The financial meltdown forced the couple to reevaluate their lives and careers. By now, they had welcomed their daughter Pacifique to the family, so a creative job search plan was essential, and that included thinking globally. Javier was from Mexico and had lived in the Netherlands while studying for his master's degree and Cordelia had lived in London and Turkey, so they were very comfortable looking for a new job anywhere in the world.

"After a year on unemployment, we were very fortunate that Javier found a job in Singapore in 2010 with an Indian-owned design firm. His former boss from the States had moved to Singapore to work for the company and decided to bring Javier over, also. The move was a bit complicated for us because I was pregnant with our second daughter, Claude, who is now four. I was actually looking forward to some time off. I had been working since I was fifteen years old and wanted the time to spend some quality time with our daughters."

They were the very first family to move into a brand new thirty-story high-rise condominium in a seven-tower complex. The constant construction noise in the beginning made it difficult to care for the children, but that soon abated and the couple began to enjoy living in Singapore. Javier's job, working in a new division that served hotel, restaurant and casino clients, was to his liking, but after several years, the prospects of a better job lured them to Bangkok.

"I had mixed feelings about leaving Singapore. It was very clean, the transportation and school systems were excellent, English was one of the national languages, it had all the modern conveniences and the food was great. Bangkok, on the other hand, was a bit of a mystery. We really did not know what to expect in Bangkok."

This time they sold or donated just about everything they had and moved to mostly Thai neighborhood close to Bangkok's business district in early 2012.

"We live on the border of the Sathorn district, near the famous Klong Toei wet market. Sathorn is a very popular area close to a lot of things, like the Bangkok Skytrain, the Chao Phraya River and a number of good restaurants. We chose the area mainly because the French school used to be located in that district and a lot of French expats still remain. We want our kids to grow up tri-lingual, speaking Spanish, French and English. Our initial idea was to put our girls into a French school. Our new area was a great location because the French International School of Bangkok buses could easily hop on the highway from this part of town."

Public transportation also was a major reason why they chose Sathorn. Bangkok's legendary traffic often requires using several modes of transportation to get to your destination. Living close to work, school or transport access points, like highway ramps, are crucial to save time and make life bearable in crowded Bangkok.

Cordelia's house is in a "mubaan," a gated cluster of homes with its own security guard. Their neighbors are Thai, not other expats. Typical of Thai homes, there is no hot water in the kitchen, only in the shower.

"We discovered that you cannot buy a house if you are a foreigner living in Thailand but you can buy a condominium. We did not want a condominium so we rented a house. The first week we moved in I met a really wonderful neighbor who spoke English and we had a nice chat. He told me, 'Do you realize that no one is going to speak to you?' He was not trying to be mean, he just wanted me to understand the reality of not speaking Thai. We did not speak Thai and not many Thais could speak English, Thais are very reserved and generally prefer not to mix. Everyone smiles and is very polite. Thailand is known as the 'land of smiles,' you know."

Renting in Thailand requires a rent deposit for the first and last months, similar to the U.S. Cordelia thinks renting is the best approach to take when living abroad because it is a much more flexible option. It allows new expats to easily move to another area if their initial home or neighborhood does not work out for them.

"If you rent, make darn sure that the contract has a 'Diplomatic Clause,' which will allow you to get out of your contract if your company decides to move you. With that clause you have the legal right to break your lease with sufficient cause."

Javier works for a local Thai firm so they did not receive a corporate expat financial package to help with their rent and allow them to enroll their kids in an international school. Restricted by money, Cordelia's plan to send the girls to a French school had to be changed.

"Sure, I would love to be able to send my kids to an international school, particularly one that would allow them to learn Spanish and French. Our goal from the start was for them to learn those languages so they could be tri-lingual. I would also like to develop a writing career as a freelance writer but that also will not happen right away. Our only option, really, was to homeschool our daughters."

Homeschooling is gaining popularity as an option for many expats, whether or not they can afford a private or international school. Cordelia also considered putting her kids in a local Thai school, but the language barrier and long hours of rote learning used in Thai schools dissuaded her.

"One thing I really like about homeschooling is that I can choose the best of a lot of different systems. I am using Singapore math and a French program for French and an English program for English. I also like the history program we are using, a kind of 'history of the world' approach. We use a combination of classical education and real world schooling."

Real world schooling includes taking the kids to an organic farm in northern Thailand for ten days to learn about the environment and whatever else they are interested in. Cordelia plans projects around whatever the kids say they want to learn.

"I try to focus on one country every six months, so right now they are learning about Mexico, their father's home. Javier lived in many areas of Mexico because his dad was a geological engineer. We teach them about the history of Mexico, the food, the plants, basically everything. I think immersion is a good way to learn."

Cordelia did a lot of online research to craft the curricula she is using, including joining online expat homeschooling groups to find out what works and what does not work. In the end, she chose programs and a style of teaching that would keep her kids curious and instill in them a love of learning.

She is also creating her own online platform - Global Homeschooling Network - to help provide a community for international homeschoolers and space to share information. She will focus on multilingual and multicultural approaches.

Her days now busy educating her children, Cordelia turned to online groups at night to forge new relationships in Bangkok.

"I found that homeschooling and kids are great ways to connect with people online. When we were In Singapore, having a baby was actually a great way to meet people in the expat community because you have a common thread. When we moved to Thailand, I went online to join women's groups and meet-up groups, to get to know local people. Wherever you go, there are always 'mommy groups.'"

When she first arrived in Bangkok, Cordelia was introduced to American, British and French expat groups that help familiarize new arrivals to the city. They helped her meet people and expand her contacts within her neighborhood, which was welcomed because of the difficulty of getting around in Bangkok.

But even with the help of expat support groups, Cordelia still feels like an outsider in Bangkok, particularly because she lacks local language skills.

"I thought it would be easier to integrate here. I think my biggest disappointment is always feeling like an outsider, feeling culturally alien. It is very different living in Thailand."

Cordelia admits that she underestimated the cultural differences she found in Bangkok and the general approach to life in Asia. She was able to handle what she calls the "surface stuff," like climate and food differences, but the deeper cultural differences have challenged her.

"In Singapore, for example, I tried to get the condo office manager to let us in the downstairs community room one day because the construction people were drilling the concrete floor in the unit above us. I had a newborn and small child and they were petrified by the deafening and dangerous noise. I could not get the people who worked in the office to let me in the community room to quiet my kids because they needed their manager's approval. They were so inflexible. The only thing they knew how to do was follow the rules. Making an independent decision did not even occur to them. In Singapore, it was all about following the rules and in Thailand, it is all about saving face."

She also finds cultural differences in her healthcare experiences. She discovered that questioning decisions made by her doctors was deemed unacceptable in a culture where authority is not questioned.

"The Thai medical system is actually quite good. As a matter of fact, Thailand is a major destination for people from around the world who come here for less expensive medical procedures. Putting the authority issue aside, we generally have been pleased with our hospital and doctors. We use one of the non-profit Catholic hospitals, not the hospitals most expats use. Expat hospitals generally are better equipped, but often charge thirty-to-forty-percent more, mainly because their employers pick up the tab. We get very good care at a much lower price."

Cultural differences have not always been negative for Cordelia, though. She admires the hidden warmth of the Thai people, particularly when it comes to children.

"Thai people will smile at you but are generally quite reserved. I found that beneath that reserve is a genuine caring for other people, especially children. I got caught in one of Bangkok's famous tropical downpours with my kids one day and was ankle deep in sewage water. A car driven by a high society-type of woman stopped and offered to take us wherever we wanted to go. That happened to us several times and was a real act of kindness."

Cordelia was so impressed by the Asian devotion to children that she wrote an article for a publication on her experiences and the lessons she had learned from living in Asia.

"The genuine love of kids is so wonderful. It means a lot to me, a mother with small children. If we were living in the U.S. or the U.K., I think it would be different. I would feel constantly judged. You do not have that here and that is really nice."

One of Cordelia's biggest complaints about living in Bangkok, like most expats, is the difficulty in getting anywhere within the city. Unlike Singapore, with its modern, efficient transportation system, Bangkok's narrow streets, rivers and nearly fifteen million people make it extremely difficult to get anywhere quickly, even with multiple modes of transportation.

"A lot of people choose not to have a car here because it is so difficult to get around. And, if you get in an accident, as a foreigner, you surely will be held responsible. You can use the Metropolitan Rapid Transit system, the elevated BTS Sky Train, riverboats, taxis or Tuk-tuks, which are very small three-wheeled vehicles, but at certain times of the day, it is hopeless. Taxis are very inexpensive here so that is what I use most of the time to get around. You just have to be very, very aware of what time of day it is. Sometimes it is just better to stay home."

Cordelia and her family look forward to escaping local traffic and getting out of Bangkok every once in a while, especially to relieve the stress that comes with Javier's often eighty-hour workweeks, common in his field. Besides the trip to the Chang Mai farm in mountainous northern Thailand, the family has visited the beautiful islands of Phuket in the Andaman Sea and Koh Samed in the Gulf of Thailand. The closest beaches to Bangkok are less than three hours by car.

Now past the three-year mark in Bangkok, Cordelia, Javier and their girls are finally settled and into the flow of daily expat life. They have no intention of ever returning to the United States. They are enjoying planning their next adventure abroad, although they do not know when. The girls are hoping for Canada or Japan whenever the time comes to move on.

"I am finally comfortable here. I do not want to move back to the U.S. I feel like it has completely lost its way. Now that I am actually out of the trees and looking back I can see the forest, and it is not what the Founding Fathers had in mind.

More Americans need to get out and live abroad. They would benefit from viewing the world from a different perspective and hopefully enjoy a better quality of life in the process. You know, I discovered that the typical ten days of vacation Americans take each year really is not enough. I am not against working hard, but are you really going to stand at the edge of your grave and say, 'Gee, I wish I had put in a few more hours at the office?' What a price to pay."

CHAPTER 7

Laurat Ogunjobi
Age 32
Manresa, Spain

"Being an expat changes your life forever. If you decide to go back to the U.S., you will not be on the same level as your peers. You will be far ahead of them because you have been exposed to a much different aspect of life."

BORN IN CHICAGO, Laurat Ogunjobi knows all about that different aspect of life as an expat living in Spain's Catalonia region. She lived for years in West Africa and now has carved out a new life for herself near Barcelona, the vibrant center of Catalan life in Spain.

Laurat's journey to life as an expat began when her parents left their home in West Africa to attend Northwestern University in the leafy Chicago suburb of Evanston. While attending school on Liberian government-funded scholarships, her birth mother gave her as a gift to a fellow Liberian scholar and his American wife, who became a great role model for Laurat throughout her life.

Her biological mother returned to Liberia to serve as a diplomat in that country's Ministry of Defense. Meanwhile, In Evanston, her adopted mother graduated with a Ph.D. in political science and her adopted father received his master's degree in transportation engineering.

Laurat's adopted father decided not to take the career path he had prepared for in college and instead decided to open to his own African arts and culture gallery in Chicago. His wife authored a book, taught part-time at the university level and raised Laurat, before joining her husband in his business.

But when Laurat reached school age, her parents decided to send her to Liberia for grade school, to better understand African culture and be with her birth mother. She enrolled Laurat in an international Episcopalian boarding school in Brewerville, forty-five minutes outside of Liberia's capital, Monrovia. Laurat also attended several private and international schools that offered a blend of British and American curricula, with generous helpings of West African culture.

"I spent the first six years of school in Liberia, which was my first exposure to my family's culture. It was quite an experience for me, and one that I will never forget. I did not realize at the time that I would one day return to West Africa."

Laurat graduated from Evanston Township High School in 1996 and then left immediately for Clark Atlanta University in Atlanta, an all-black school.

"I went there because I wanted an all-black experience at college, but after a year, I decided that what I really wanted was a career in art communications and I could not get what I wanted at Clark. I switched schools to the Atlanta Art Institute and graduated in 2000 with a bachelor's degree in visual communications. Looking back on it now, it was definitely the right thing to do."

Laurat returned to her hometown and started her first job as the director of communications for the Chicago-area office of the non-profit organization, the Association of Community Organizations for Reform Now (ACORN).

"It was a very good position for me considering I was right out of college. It did not pay well but it gave me the title and exposure I needed to advance my career."

But life changed dramatically for Laurat after just two years in her new job.

"When I was living in Atlanta, I met and fell in love with Geah, who was Liberian. We got married in 2001 after we returned to Chicago. A year later, I convinced him that I was ready to leave the ACORN job to move to Liberia. We believed that the government there was becoming much more stable and many government jobs and U.N.-funded opportunities were beginning to open up, which was our primary interest for moving there."

The couple moved to Monrovia and Laurat found a job working for a local newspaper. But soon Geah became frustrated with Liberia's government bureaucracy and poor infrastructure and made it clear he wanted to leave. They returned to Chicago in less than a year and divorce followed soon after.

Still trying to cope with the unrest in her life, Laurat turned once again to a job in the communications industry. She went to work for Purple Monkey Studios, an interactive media company in Chicago that created educational technology modules. But the job did not last long. The lure of an expat life pulled her back to West Africa after just a year.

"By now my divorce was final and I needed to clear my head, so I packed my bags and headed for Nigeria this time, the land of my biological father. I loved it so much I stayed for six months, mainly living off my savings. I also lived in Ghana for a few months. They had a very stable economy and lots of things were going on there. This is when I started entertaining the idea of becoming a long-term expat."

But soon her savings ran out and Laurat needed to return to her hometown to find a new job. She quickly landed one with Multimedia Sales and Marketing as a media consultant in 2010.

"This is really when it started, after I got back this time from West Africa. I said to myself: 'You know what? I want to start looking for something to do that will allow me to live out of the United States.' I loved being an expat and wanted to explore the world."

That something became her current company, Cush Consulting Group, which provides mainly marketing and communications expertise to a variety of firms. Her very first client provided Laurat with the opportunity to return to West Africa. The company needed someone to help them establish a business in Ghana. She met with lawyers there to incorporate the business and lay the groundwork for the company's arrival.

Now armed with consulting experience, Laurat began bidding aggressively for new project work and landed several big fish.

"I became the go-to marketing communications consultant for the Chicago-area. First, I helped Google launch its Chromebook product and then Samsung asked me to help roll out its new Galaxy Experience into retail kiosks."

Her business and lifestyle aspirations finally began to merge in the summer of 2012 when she snagged an assignment with Rail Europe, which markets the popular Eurail Pass for train travel throughout the European continent.

"When I got that job I started visiting Europe frequently and taking vacations there. I was part of the website team responsible for providing consumer information. Actually, one of the great things about this assignment was that part of my pay at the end of the project was free rail tickets.

I went to Italy for the first time and really fell in love with Milan. I started thinking about how cool it would be to live in Europe."

But Laurat had some concerns about moving to Europe. Most of her experience living abroad had been in West Africa. She felt safer and more comfortable there because everyone looked like her and she had experience living there. She knew the culture and the customs. But after traveling through Europe by rail, Laurat began developing more confidence in her ability to live in a more unfamiliar setting.

"Once I convinced myself I could do it, I started checking online employment websites in Denmark, Germany, Italy and a few other countries, but I did not receive a lot of responses. About that time, though, I was fortunate to receive a large sum of money and said to myself, 'Now is the time for me to really look at going to Europe.' I started sending emails to companies and following up with old contacts that could help. Finally, several companies in Spain began responding to me, asking when I was coming and saying they could use me right away."

One of the people she heard from owned an English-language radio station for the expat community in Spain. The owner was interested in offering Laurat a job as an on-air presenter, but Laurat was not interested. She continued to explore other employment possibilities in Spain, although the job market presented challenges.

"Spain has a very high unemployment rate, particularly among young people. One of the problems is the mismatch between education and the type of new jobs being created there. There are too many unskilled or skilled workers with little education chasing jobs that require a lot more education. Since Spanish firms are competing in the global marketplace, they are looking for well-educated, experienced workers, particularly those who are fluent in English. I discovered that there are a lot of companies in Spain looking for people like me to help them market to the expat community."

She found several and with a large check she had just received, boarded a plane in Chicago and flew to Barcelona in early 2014 to open the first Cush Consulting Group international office. Her consulting business would now focus on international marketing and communications for education, philanthropic causes and cultural initiatives.

"I really did not do a lot of research before I landed in Barcelona, primarily because I was fortunate to have a friend in Chicago who had a tour guide friend living in Barcelona. He helped me do everything when I arrived."

He also soon became Laurat's second husband. From Ghana, Ibrahim had lived in Barcelona for seven years and guided Laurat through all the steps necessary to start her new life in Spain.

"He did all the planning for me, which made my transition very easy. I had to use a lawyer, though, to get my national tax identification number (NIE) and visa. You need them to work in Spain, open a bank account, rent a home and lots of other things."

From the start, Laurat learned that lawyers could be very helpful in Spain, a country where everything, it seems, requires a contract.

"Everyone has an employment contract in Spain, even bartenders. And each contract has to be stamped by an employer with their stamp to be legal. Even a rental house requires a contract stamped by the landlord."

Although Laurat's new clients were located in Barcelona, she chose to live in Manresa, a small city of more than seventy-five thousand people located in the geographic center of Catalonia, about forty-miles northwest of Barcelona.

"I could have lived closer to my clients, but it is so beautiful here in the mountains and it is only a little over an hour by train to Barcelona. Since

I go into the city just every other day, it made sense. Paying less than four hundred dollars a month for our one-bedroom apartment also made sense. If we had rented in Barcelona, we would have paid twice as much. We love our apartment with its old, classical feel. I love that old-fashioned look."

When in Barcelona, Laurat works out of the office of her largest client, a Spanish company that sells insurance policies to expats. She handles business development and marketing communications to help them reach the expat community in Spain. She also works with Zeno Radio, a New York firm that streams international radio stations to expats around the world.

"Zeno is an interesting company that has tapped into a great niche audience. They are expanding into Europe and I did their market testing in Spain."

Laurat also works with a cultural exchange group to help prepare Spanish high school students for exchange programs in English-speaking countries. She teaches them English and prepares them for their new cultural experience, primarily in the United States, but also works with a few who are headed to the United Kingdom."

Living in smaller and somewhat more isolated Manresa has given Laurat an opportunity to learn Spanish and Catalan from the locals. English is not spoken much in Manresa, mainly because it receives far fewer tourists than Barcelona and few expats live there. The tiny community of expats are mainly British, German, Russian, Romanian, Latin American, Moroccan and from other African countries.

"Manresa has a lot of Moroccan shops that sell very well-priced foods and it is all organic and very healthy. I especially like that they sell halal meat, because I am Muslim. Halal is Islamic butchered meat, much like the kosher meat for Orthodox Jews. I spend about thirty dollars every two weeks for food and produce, which is amazing. The food is so good here that I have actually put on about fifteen pounds since moving here."

Spain's lower cost of living also extends to Laurat's healthcare needs. Being married to Ibrahim, a permanent resident of Spain, allows her to use the country's national healthcare program at no cost. Dental care, though, is another matter. Like most expats living in Spain, she must pay for private dental insurance, although it is very inexpensive, about six dollars a month.

Laurat and Ibrahim also love the Spanish lifestyle, with its focus on family and friends and more leisurely attitudes toward life and work.

"It is a very different, more accepting atmosphere here, I think, than the United States. I am a black woman and a Muslim, which I began practicing after my divorce. I wear a head veil and no one seems to mind at all. They are very family-oriented in Spain and naturally very warm people. It also is a very different work culture than I was used to. It is definitely not a 'mind your own business' environment. Spaniards do not separate their business life from their social and family lives, which makes life far more relaxed."

The typical Spanish tradition of closing businesses in the early afternoon for a long, leisurely meal with family is very appealing to Laurat, although she is still getting used to the practice of having the evening meal late in the day, often after ten at night.

"I definitely get it when people refer to Spain as 'Europe's night owls.' Businesses close in early afternoon and re-open around five or six in the evening and then close again around nine or ten. That is when things really start going, often lasting well past midnight every day of the week. When I first moved here, Ibrahim and I would join the crowd and stay up late but not so much anymore."

Laurat also admires the Spanish attitude toward money and their joy of life.

"Spaniards love to have a good time but money is only a part it. They get great joy out of the simple things in life, like walking with friends and family. I love that, in Barcelona, there is bench to sit on in every single block in the city, some designed by the famous Barcelona architect, Gaudi. Everywhere you look, there is a bench to rest and visit with family, friends and meet new people. I really love that."

Outside of work, Laurat has mainly expat friends because of her limited language skills. She belongs to a number of different expat groups with shared interests, like paddle tennis, start-up ventures and young professionals. She also has started to increase her visibility in the Barcelona expat community through the meet-up groups she and her husband attend, which has been good for both her business and social lives.

Laurat's Spanish friends are still limited primarily to business colleagues and clients, although her circle of friends has widened a bit through Ibrahim's job with Grupo Antolin, a Spanish automobile manufacturer. Ibrahim has lived in Spain for nearly eight years and has developed a number of friendships through his work.

"Life would be so much easier for any expat coming here if they would just learn at least some Spanish. What frustrates so many expats is the red tape and bureaucracy and, of course, everything is in Spanish. There are no dual language documents in Spain. If you do not know the language, it can be a big problem. In America, they find a way to accommodate people who do not speak English as their first language, but here there is very little accommodation. The people who make it here know Spanish and also are well educated. If you do not have both, this is probably not the place to be."

Laurat had the education but lacked language skills when she came to Spain. With Ibrahim's help, though, she has managed to minimize the culture shock and integration problems that often occur when expats touch down in an unfamiliar distant land.

"I am still definitely getting used to the 'military time' they use here. I always have to ask my husband, 'What is seventeen-thirty again?' I think I need a little chart to carry around to help me remember what the actual time is. I also am not at all thrilled with the lack of professionalism I see from service people in Spain. In America, service is usually pretty good. If I am spending money, I want to receive good service wherever I live. It just seems to not be a priority here. I guess you just have to take the bad with the good. If you want Spain's laid-back lifestyle, you have to realize that it often can come with lousy service."

Her concerns with customer service melt away when she begins talking about the bountiful sunshine and mild climate of her new home.

"The weather is just so wonderful here all of the time. I am still getting used to people being outside almost every day, just sitting or dining on their terrazas. Believe me, it is a nice change from that wicked Chicago weather."

With both her business and personal life humming along, Laurat believes she made a great choice in deciding to live in Catalonia and embrace the life of an American abroad in Spain.

"I am not interested in going back to the United States at all. My husband sometimes talks about moving to Germany, but I tell him, 'Dude, come on. We should buy property here and use this as our European base.' Even if we should move temporarily to Germany or Dubai or some of the other places he talks about, we would always have a base in Spain. You know, I have a great lifestyle here without busting my butt. What else do you want?"

CHAPTER 8

— ❧ —

Will Martinez
Age 22
Rio de Janeiro, Brazil

"The idea of returning to Rio did not really hit me until I got home from my trip. I really loved that place and wanted to go back. About a month or two before graduation, I was not sure what I wanted to do with my life, so I decided to look at the things I really love, like travel and writing and meeting new people. I also like to teach and thought that might be a good way to get back to Brazil."

SOUTH AMERICA HAD always fascinated Will Martinez but his family's annual vacation never seemed to include Latin America. While working in his school's study abroad office during the fall semester of 2013, though, he ran across an international relations study program in Rio de Janeiro that finally held the promise of travel to the continent that he dreamed about. The month Will spent in Rio the following January decided his destiny.

Born in Philadelphia and raised in Greenville, Delaware, an affluent suburb of Wilmington, Will and his younger brother grew up living the life of an upper-middle class family, playing tennis and golf and excelling in school. His father is a long-time client representative for IBM and his mother, who also worked at IBM for a while, is an elementary teacher. Will's grandparents owned a travel agency, which allowed the family to often travel internationally.

After high school graduation, Will chose to attend exclusive Hofstra University on Long Island for its communications program and its proximity to New York City.

"Coming from a small town of about two thousand people, I was always fascinated with New York. That whole fast-paced lifestyle really appealed to me. Hofstra seemed perfect for me because it was just seven miles from New York City and had a very good school of communication. I had a double major of public relations and global studies, with a minor in drama."

While in school, Will got a job in Hofstra's study abroad office and found the idea of living and studying in another country very interesting, especially since one of his majors was global studies. He had never been to South America, so he spent much of his time researching education opportunities in Brazil and Argentina. In the winter session of his last semester at Hofstra, he found a one-month program called "Summit Global Education" that seemed promising.

"Since I worked in the office I had access to a lot of resources and information about different countries. I started researching South America by looking at the culture, history, music, the people and even the films of Brazil and Argentina. Summit had an international relations program in Rio de Janeiro for the month of January that attracted my attention. It was going to be held at ESPM, which is a marketing and communications school in Rio. The program seemed so perfect for what I wanted and it also was my chance to finally get to visit South America."

When he was not in class at ESPM, Will explored the city and its surroundings and loved what he saw, particularly the marriage of Rio's magnificent natural setting with the pulsating energy of the carioca people. It reminded him of what he liked about big cities. When he flew home in early February, Will left a part of himself in Rio de Janeiro.

"I started thinking a lot about Rio and maybe going back there, probably around late March or early April. It is about that time when all college students who are facing graduation ask themselves: 'What am I going to do with my life?' At that point, I did not know what I was going to do but I began to feel that whatever it was, I was going to do it in Rio."

During his final spring semester at Hofstra, Will interned for an online company that wrote blogs and reviews about movies that were closely related to a travel location. For example, Woody Allen's *Midnight in Paris* was linked to extensive travel information on Paris for travelers thinking about visiting the French capital.

Will was assigned mainly writing and social media work, a nice mesh of his talents and his public relations major at school. The job also helped ignite his passion for travel and adventure, and pointed him even more strongly toward Rio.

"I started researching Brazil again, this time for something I could do down there to make a living. At first I was looking for community service projects. I thought I might be able to do something through ESPM, the school I had attended in January. But that turned out to be a dead end because it did not pay a lot of money."

It was Will's schoolteacher mother who came up with the idea to teach in Brazil, which made perfect sense to Will since he was considering teaching as a career option.

"I had thought a lot about teaching, even going back to school for an advanced degree so I could teach at the university level. So when mom mentioned teaching to me, I wanted to know more about it. Then I ran into a girl who had graduated from high school with me who was working for goabroad.com, a website that helps people find Teaching English as a Foreign Language (TEFL) certification programs so they can work abroad. She suggested that I contact the International TEFL Academy, which had a well-regarded TEFL certification program. It was more expensive than many of the other programs I had researched, but the guy I spoke with really knew his stuff and showed a lot of concern for me. He told me that TEFL could actually be a lifetime job for me, if I wanted it to be."

Will started his TEFL certification program a month or so before he graduated from Hofstra and finally completed it by early July. All of his TEFL classes were online, except for required in-class teaching experience. He also opted for an additional two-week module for teaching English to business people.

"I also had to spend twenty hours of in-class teaching, tutoring or observing to get my certification. To satisfy that requirement, I found a volunteer group in Delaware that taught English to non-native speakers during weeknights. I just sat and observed the first two classes but then had my own class after that. I had anywhere from three to six students, depending on the night. One guy was from Peru, two were from South Korea, two from India and one from Pakistan. Teaching that class really helped my confidence."

After he finished all of his TEFL certification requirements, Will contacted the company's advisor for South America. She gave him a list of about fifteen companies in Rio de Janeiro that taught English and also helped him prepare his international resume.

After he finished his TEFL certification program, Will continued his summer job of teaching tennis to youngsters at a local community center in Greenville while he waited to hear from the companies he had been contacting in Rio. He did not have to wait long.

"My parents had gotten me a roundtrip ticket to Rio for my graduation present, which could not have been better since I knew that I would have to actually be there to find a job. Even better, my father decided that we should all go to Rio in early August, including my younger brother, who is going to school at Colgate University. The plan was for all of us to spend ten days together and then I would stay for several more months to find a job there."

"My plan was to tour Brazil with my family but I ended up doing a lot of job interviewing during our stay in Rio. I was lucky to land a job right away with New Start Communications, a company that has been doing business in Rio for over twenty-five years. New Start provides TEFL teachers to businesses that want their employees to know English. Classes are held either at the client's place of business or at the New Start offices in Rio."

One of New Start's largest clients is a multinational French cement company, which prefers teachers from New Start because it provides primarily American, Australian and British English-speakers. The French company had been dissatisfied with other companies that offered mainly Brazilian English teachers.

Before Will started teaching he was not given any formal training by New Start, although the company thoroughly briefed him on each of his students. He was told their teaching preferences, the type of book they wanted to use, whether or not they liked the use of supplemental video programs and other individual preferences to help him customize the learning experience for each student. The company also prepared Will's first lesson plan.

By his fourth lesson, Will felt confident enough to not ask the company for help, except for special situations or questions. He mainly tutored individual clients, who are mostly business people from companies like the consulting firm KPMG and the oil giant, Chevron. He also taught English to an accountant at a hotel in Copacabana. Most of the classes he taught were held either at the client's work place or home.

"Because they all work from nine to five every day, my classes usually are scheduled around their work day. I have one student at eight in the morning, some around the lunch hour and a few after five. It can get to be a long day when you have an early morning client and an early evening client during the same day."

Soon after Will began working for New Start, he went online and found a place to live that was located in Rio's Lagoa neighborhood, an upscale area in the south zone with lots of places for him to just hang out.

"The website I used is mostly for people who want to rent a room in their apartment, which was fine for me. For the first few months, I stayed in a woman's apartment with two other people, a Brazilian and a Brit, both students. We all had separate bedrooms but shared a bathroom, a kitchen and a living room. The location of the apartment was really great. It was situated on the Lagoa, which is a big lake in the south part of Rio. Every morning I got up and walked by the lake. Lagoa also has a lot of things going on most of the time."

The cooperative living arrangement worked well for Will. His monthly rent for his shared accommodations was around five hundred dollars a month, a real bargain, considering the affluence of his new neighborhood.

But his stay in Lagoa turned out to be temporary. By mid-November, Will moved to Rio's busy Copacabana district in the heart of Rio, just two blocks from the beach and surrounded by hotels, restaurants and bars.

"The apartment is actually my friend's apartment. I met him last January when I was studying at ESPM. He is traveling for a while and is letting me rent his apartment while he is abroad, which is a really good deal for me. I pay about six hundred and fifty dollars a month for a great place just two blocks from Copacabana Beach and in the middle of everything that is going on in Rio."

The apartment is just one bedroom, but it has a large queen-size bed and a large cabinet. Quite spacious for a Rio apartment, it has a living room, kitchen and bath with a shower, but lacks a washer and a dryer.

"I have to go out to do my laundry, which is a real bummer. But I really do not mind that much because I am so close to the beach and in the middle of everything. There is no sea view from the apartment but I do have a nice view of the mountains that ring Rio."

Will is always on the go and finds many things to do in Rio. He especially likes the nearby beach and the Tijuca Forest, a tropical rainforest that is thought to be the largest urban forest in the world. It is home to hundreds of species of plants and wildlife that are only found in the Atlantic rainforest.

"Tijuca forest is so beautiful and it is does not cost anything to get in. I often ride my bike there or take a bus and just hike all day. One of the cool things about Tijuca is the number of waterfalls within the park. I think there are about thirty. Brazilians like to go to the waterfalls and swim under them. It is a really cool and popular thing to do. A really nice waterfall is about a thirty-minute hike from the entrance I use."

Will also likes to hike up a hill that has a spectacular view of Rio's iconic Sugarloaf Mountain, a peak that juts nearly thirteen hundred feet above Rio's Guanabara Bay.

"It takes about forty-five minutes to get to the top of the hill but when you get there, the view is unbelievable. It takes me about ten minutes by bike and five minutes by bus to get there. Once I start climbing, I find monkeys and lizards and all sorts of other animals. It is so cool."

Another of Will's favorite pastimes is going to samba parties at night and on weekends to hear the rhythms of Brazil's national dance, brought to the country five centuries ago by slaves and freed slaves, mostly from Africa.

"The band members sit in a circle, playing and singing and then people start dancing the samba. Everyone there knows the songs and sings along while they dance. The samba parties are held everywhere in Rio almost every night. You find out about them online or through friends. I am really looking forward to my first Rio carnival in February. All of the samba groups throughout Rio compete against each other."

Will travels around the city mainly by bus and Rio's subway system, Metrô Rio. Bus transportation, though, does not get high marks from either Will or locals.

"There are a ton of buses here but I hear a lot of complaints. Most people think the bus drivers are crazy. Sometimes your bus does not come and if it does, it often takes a long time. The good news is that buses go everywhere in Rio and they are cheap. I usually pay only a dollar to go most anywhere in the city. If I take the Metro, it costs me about fifty cents more. For me, that is not a bad deal. But local people get very upset."

After living in Brazil for a number of months, Will is beginning to see the economy and the cost of living in Rio through the eyes of Brazilians, who are very concerned with government spending on the 2014 World Cup, and the Olympic Games, which are scheduled to be held in Rio in the summer of 2016. Prices have gone up in the country to help fund those events and inflation is on the rise once again.

He discusses these issues with his friends, who are mainly Brazilians. Unlike many expats, Will has not done a lot of online socializing to develop American expat friendships, relying more on people he has met through work or just by hanging out in Rio.

"I am friends with a few teachers but I do not know any Americans. My good friends are from England and Mexico and I also have lots of Brazilian friends. When I studied here last January I made some friends, then they introduced me to their friends. Brazilians are very friendly people, which has allowed me to easily make friends when I go to the beach or parties."

Part of the reason Will has been so adept at developing friendships in Rio is his ability to communicate in Portuguese, Brazil's national language. He took Spanish in high school and Italian in college, which helped, but not with Portuguese pronunciation, which is somewhat difficult. He is not fluent in the language but is getting there quickly.

"I have a few friends that I hang out with that speak English. I tend to speak English with them and Portuguese with my other friends. If your friends do not speak English, you are forced to speak their language and that is when you really learn it."

He looked into Portuguese language lessons when he first moved to Rio but they were expensive and did not fit into his work schedule. Besides his Portuguese-only conversations with his Brazilian friends, Will also learns by listening to Brazilian music and then looking up the lyrics. He also watches movies in Portuguese to improve his pronunciation.

His use of the local language has helped him avoid much of the culture shock expats feel when moving to a new country, but not entirely. He discovered that Rio was a world apart from where he had come from.

"I was not prepared for the extreme poverty that you see in Rio's favelas, or slums. I came from a very upper-middle class neighborhood and was initially jolted by what I saw. I am also getting used to the street crime in the city. You sometimes see packs of kids just grab things from people right in the middle of the day. I was on the beach and all of a sudden everyone started standing up, grabbing their stuff and running away. A gang of about ten young kids just swept over the beach stealing phones, jewelry and anything they could lay their hands on. In Portuguese, this type of crime is called an 'arrastão,' or dragnet."

While Will enjoys his life in Rio, a few things still bother him, like the incessant standing in line for almost everything, even when he goes to clubs.

"Here, you have to pay a tab before you can leave a club. They give you a slip when you enter the place and then keep a tab on how much you spend. When you are ready to leave, you have to stand in a line to pay your bill before you can leave."

But like most Brazilians, Will now takes these differences in stride and does not let them bother him.

"In the U.S., people take what they have for granted. In Brazil, people are given a lot less and expect a lot less. They just deal with it and say: 'Hey, we have our samba, we have our beaches and we have the beauty of our natural surroundings. Ah, just look at this place.' It is a great attitude to have."

Will does not have an annual contract with his company, nor does he have a Brazilian work permit visa. Like other employees of the company, he remains in Brazil on a tourist visa, which must be renewed after three months.

"I have renewed once and will have an opportunity to renew another six months after that. But then you have to wait a full year before you can reapply, which is a big problem if you want to stay here and work long-term. What most people do is just over-stay their tourist visa and pay the penalty, which is around three hundred and twenty dollars."

Staying in Brazil is not a big concern for Will, although he loves living in Rio. A friend of his, who also worked for New Start, is now living in Uruguay and has told Will that jobs are plentiful there and the cost of living is much cheaper.

"I think Uruguay is definitely my next stop after Rio. Since I am not on a contract and now have the teaching experience, I can pretty much go wherever I want to. I am also thinking about teaching in Argentina and Chile. I feel like everything I have learned and the experience I have now has really changed me. You see things so differently when you live abroad and I want to continue to do that."

CHAPTER 9

Jessica Sueiro
Age 42
Curridabat, Costa Rica

"This is our first run with expat life. Although that summer in Paris was more than a vacation, it still was just temporary. Now we live full-time in Costa Rica. We both work remotely, our kids are being educated here and we have finally settled in. This is our life now. We are first-time expats and we love it."

THAT PARIS ADVENTURE in the summer of 2013 changed the arc of Jessica Sueiro's life story more than she could have ever imagined.

Jessica and her forty-four-year-old husband, Will, had been dreaming about the expat life for more than a decade. Once, earlier in Will's career, an opportunity to live in another country came up within his company, but it did not work out for them at that time. Disappointed, they tucked away their dream, raised their two kids and pursued their careers.

But their vision of living abroad would not go away.

"The travel bug was still there for us, so in 2013 Will started exploring expat positions in Europe through his company in Boston. Unfortunately, the economy was still bad there, so nothing came of it. Finally I said to him, 'The kids speak French and I want to take them to Paris for the summer. If we are not going to go through the company for a couple of years, at least let me take them to Paris for the summer.'"

Always a good planner, Jessica began developing a careful, realistic budget they could live on in Paris for several months. Then she went online and found a one-bedroom apartment through Airbnb, the online rental marketplace, that would fit her budget. Not wanting to be left behind, Will asked his employer if he could work remotely from Paris for part of the summer and, much to Will's surprise, they agreed to the plan.

"The apartment was small with problematic plumbing but we loved it. It was Paris! We had seven fabulous weeks there and, although our daughter got mononucleosis that summer, we had such a great time as a family in one of the most interesting and exciting places on the planet."

When Jessica and her family returned home to Cambridge, Massachusetts, the idea of living abroad began to transition from a dream to a plan. She told Will that moving abroad through his company was probably not going to work out and it was time to develop a plan to make it happen.

"I said, 'How long do we hold on before we can make this happen? Our kids are getting older and it will become more difficult the older they are.' That September, we developed a twelve-month plan to move abroad and set an objective to live in another country within a year."

Jessica admits that it was an aggressive plan.

"Looking back at it now, I would recommend to anyone that you give yourself at least a year and a half to two years for planning your move. It takes a lot of research and planning to get it right."

She was very thorough, researching online every aspect of moving to another country and then living there. They spent the next year selling most of their things, researching credit cards to find one that did not charge foreign fees, investigating how banking is done in other countries, finding out what medical insurance coverage would be available and the costs and the myriad of other things she knew they would need in their new life.

Jessica's initial intention was to move to France. Their summer in Paris was still fresh in their memories and both kids, seven-year-old Largo and ten-year-old Avalon, were fluent in French, so it made a lot of sense to them. But, examined in the cold light of a poor economy in France and a high cost of living there, they began to look elsewhere.

"When we started looking for a country to move to, it was less about what intrigued us and more about our budget, and that is the truth of it. I have an artist's income, which is not making us rich and my husband, who is an accountant, was planning to start his own business. Money had to be a big concern for us."

Research began on Central American countries, primarily because the cost of living was low and most were generally safe for Americans. Jessica initially chose Guatemala because the country's capital, Guatemala City, had a very good French school, which was an important criterion for the family. They took the first step south by enrolling the kids in school and began making a specific plan to move. But at the last minute, they changed their minds when their research showed a lack of Internet security in the country, particularly when transmitting financial data. Since Will planned to start a new accounting business that would be dependent on the Internet, they switched course.

"It was a big concern for us, so we changed our plan and began researching Costa Rica, which seemed to have all we wanted. It was affordable and had a French school in San José, the capital of Costa Rica. It also was one of the most bio-diverse countries in the world and, importantly for us, had a better communications infrastructure than Guatemala. Plus, we wanted our kids to have this kind of adventure, a nature experience where they could learn by observing Costa Rica's rich wildlife, rain forests and other natural wonders. We also discovered that it was one of the safest Central American countries."

Prior to making their move, they sold about eighty percent of the belongings they had accumulated in their spacious two-bedroom home in Cambridge. They kept a small storage unit for just those things the family felt were important but not necessary to take with them. Since the plan was to live in Costa Rica for just a year or two, they brought only the necessities, packed into two full suitcases and two carry-on bags for each member of the family.

"When we decided to move to Costa Rica we wanted to live simply. We knew we could live with very little because we did it in Paris for nearly two months. By taking everything with us on the plane, we saved a lot of money not having to use an international shipping company to transport our things. We also had family bring things with them when they came down to visit."

The family touched down in San José in the summer of 2014 to begin their expat life in Curridabat, a suburb seven miles east of the sprawling city of over two million people high in Costa Rica's Central Valley. Curridabat was their choice because it fit their budget and put them within a fifteen-minute drive of the French school their son Largo would attend. The area also had very few expats and English was seldom spoken, important to Jessica because blending into the local community and learning the culture was a must.

"Curridabat was a good choice, but if school had not been a major factor, we definitely would have lived some other place in the country like the Monteverde Cloud Forest or somewhere a little more rural and less Americanized."

Settling in Curridabat, Jessica quickly found that having Spanish language skills would be very important to the family's success as expats.

"It was no problem for Will because he was raised in Miami and speaks Spanish fluently. The kids are beginning to learn the language well, but I struggle with it. I work a lot of hours in my job each week and it is hard to find time to devote to learning a new language."

She found a young local girl who wanted to learn English in return for teaching Jessica Spanish, and about the country's culture. To supplement her face-to-face local learning, she also uses Duolingo, an online language program. Jessica is making progress, but like many Americans abroad, still is not fluent.

As with their sojourn to Paris, Jessica used Airbnb to find a place to rent before they arrived in Costa Rica.

"It started out as our temporary home until we found something more permanent, but once we were in it for a month we thought it would be a nice place to stay long term. I would highly recommend this approach for anyone considering a move abroad."

They asked the owners of a three-story house about renting the ground floor unit for a year and they agreed. It was perfect because the owners lived on the second and third floors of the building but owned a hotel on the Caribbean side of Costa Rica and were away often. And they spoke English very well.

"One of the reasons why I love this place is because it is one-stop shopping. We pay a monthly fee that includes both our rent and utilities. It is much less hassle that way. Each day we rise to the sound of the birds and the rushing river below our apartment. I start my day on the terrace overlooking the river with a wonderful cup of Costa Rican coffee. The birds serenade me each morning and the weather seems to be always perfect."

Largo's private French school has lived up to expectations and he is progressing well, although the promised 15-minute drive often turns into a half hour in San José's notoriously slow traffic.

For Avalon, Jessica has opted for homeschooling, a common, less expensive education option used by expats worldwide.

"I actually call it 'worldschooling,' a combination of book learning and learning from the world. We use a variety of different education philosophies married to real-world experiences. Avalon is learning about Costa Rican culture, local dance, Spanish, French, different styles of food and even a much different approach to math, which includes learning all about the local currency."

Jessica and Will designed Avalon's "worldschooling" program around education philosophies they researched, from International Baccalaureate (IB) to Waldorf to Charlotte Mason, all well-known homeschooling programs intended to place emphasis on a rounded, global education for their child.

"Avalon is one-hundred percent kinesthetic and a really avid reader, so we selected programs that worked with that and then customized them to work specifically for her needs. She has a French program, for example, which was developed by the French Ministry of Education for homeschooling. She uses a local tutor for Spanish. Avalon helps shape the program by letting us know what is working for her and what is not."

The first three months of living in Costa Rica were a tough transition for Jessica. Adjusting to a new life of homeschooling for Avalon, Largo's new school, Will's new business and the family's unfamiliarity with a completely different culture posed challenges.

"Every night we would go to bed thinking: 'I hope tomorrow is easier.' We were working seven days a week, setting up our technology needs, dealing with school stuff, buying a car and just trying to get settled. We barely left the house, but now we are finally getting to a 'new normal' for us, which finally allows us to actually get out and experience Costa Rica."

They began exploring Costa Rica through weekend family trips to the Pacific beaches, about a three-hour drive away. The Caribbean, a somewhat more tortuous five-hour drive, depending on the traffic and weather, also is a favorite family destination.

"The roads in Costa Rica are pretty bad. We found ourselves on narrow roads that were quite scary and structurally unsafe. It is also not easy to predict if you will be re-routed on a dirt road for several hours because of construction or traffic."

Family weekends exploring their new country were not the only trips made by the family. The Sueiros live in Costa Rica on tourist visas, which expire every ninety days. By Costa Rican law, they must visit another country, so far Nicaragua and Guatemala. Then they must return to have their passports stamped by Costa Rica Immigration to remain in the country for another three-month period.

"We actually tried to get long-term visas when we were still living in the U.S., but were told by the consulate in New York that we could not get student visas for our kids. We were petrified because we were just two months away from moving to Costa Rica. We checked a lot of online communities and discovered that living in a country on a tourist visa is a fairly common expat practice. Since we do not plan to remain here for more than two years, it seemed like a sensible solution, and it has been."

Jessica views the 90-day trips to surrounding countries as just another adventure for her and her family, not an inconvenience.

Daily life in Curridabat is not all work and school. Jessica has made integrating into the local community a priority and her social life reflects that. She has made some local expat friends, but she does not spend a lot of time with them, especially American expats.

"We feel that spending most of our time with other expats would interfere with our integration into the local culture. We moved here for the cultural experience and that means developing relationships with Costa Ricans, or Ticos, as they are called. That does not mean we do not have any expat friends, though. I actually love helping newcomers to Costa Rica. I am so inspired by people who are taking the plunge."

Jessica has met many Ticos through Largo's French school, which is mainly attended by Costa Rican students, and through Avalon's dance class.

"She takes a traditional Costa Rican dance class, which happened on a fluke. We were at the local farmer's market and my daughter saw girls dancing and said she would like to join them. The instructor agreed and it has been a wonderful experience for her and for us. You can learn so much from other cultures just by participating in social events like a dance class. You know, people tend to be so judgmental when they get in their bubble and often become negative about their experience in the country. We tried to avoid that. I find it refreshing that we have been so welcomed here. People are eager to learn about us and we about them."

But social life often has had to take a back seat to work for Jessica and Will. She has been a graphic designer for over two decades, ever since graduating from Syracuse University in New York with a B.S. in photography. She started her own business – Cucumber Design – in Los Angeles, designing marketing materials mainly for large, corporate clients. Over the years, her business has grown into an international design studio that develops branding and corporate identification materials for start-ups to large corporations.

"I met Will at a trade show when I was living in L.A. and he was in Florida working for a cruise line. We both traveled a lot and had many frequent flier miles, so we started a two-year long-distance romance that ended in 2000 when we both moved to New York and decided to get married."

Will graduated from Fordham University with a B.S. in accounting and the two moved west to Los Angeles, started a family and then returned to the Boston-area, not far from Maine, where Jessica was born and raised.

Although Jessica was a twenty-year veteran of owning and operating her own design business, easily transportable to Costa Rica via the Internet and modern communication tools, Will was on his own for the first time.

"Will started his accounting business when we moved here. It is a U.S. Limited Liability Company (LLC). We are not citizens of Costa Rica so everything is run through the U.S. We pay taxes to the U.S. on our income and have U.S. bank accounts. We have not entertained the idea of working for local customers mainly because we would then have to pay local taxes. We are quite happy with working with clients based in the U.S. and using our income here because the cost of living is so much lower."

Jessica admits that working from home is a mixed blessing. She and Will put in long hours each day and often weekends and holidays, but both agree that not missing a moment of their kids' childhood and the improved work/life balance is well worth it.

With both businesses humming and happy kids, life, as they say in Costa Rica, is *pura vida* for Jessica and her family.

"We came here for the adventure and the cultural experience and I am happy to say that it is all we had hoped for. Although we have been here for a relatively short period of time, we really feel like we belong. We are also pretty stoked about reducing our cost of living by about two-thirds, which has allowed us to wipe away a small amount of debt, save some money and think about future real estate investments."

Jessica also loves the near-perfect weather of Costa Rica's Central Valley, a big departure from Boston's cold, snowy winters, even with the long rainy period that greens the valley. And now that the family finally is settled, they are beginning to sample the abundance of Costa Rica's wildlife, beaches, mountains and rainforests.

There are a few blemishes, though, on their *pura vida* lifestyle. Jessica does not like what she calls "gringo pricing," the local practice of inflating prices for tourists and expats, a common practice throughout the world. She cannot understand why someone who contributes to the local economy should pay a higher price for the same thing locals buy for a lesser amount.

But a few blemishes do not dampen Jessica's ardor for her adopted new country.

"Our first three months here were awful. I cried everyday. But I can tell you that it was the best decision we ever made. We now want to figure out how we can continue to do this for the next ten years, at least."

Jessica is convinced that if she could become an expat in her early forties, anyone can do it.

"Most people do not make a move mainly because of fear. Fear of how they are going to make money, fear of how they are going to educate their kids, fear their kids are going to miss out on something. We all have those same struggles because it is not easy being away from family and friends. What I will tell you is that we have become better parents, better educated and the move has enhanced our marriage. It took us a long time to get to this point. Overcome your fears and just do it. We waited too long."

The adventure will continue for Jessica and Will. They are already planning a move to Ecuador, sometime within the next year.

CHAPTER 10

Lauren Kicknosway
Age 44
Sydney, Australia

"Being an expat is such a different experience than traveling or even slow traveling, where people rent apartments and stay for a while. When I go somewhere I want to dig in, I want to go grocery shopping, discover the hidden spots and be there for a while."

THE GIRL FROM Bloomfield Hills, Michigan got her expat wish fulfilled when both she and her husband were offered jobs in Sydney, Australia over six years ago.

Lauren was born and raised in the Detroit suburbs, but at sixteen her mom, a junior college English professor and poet, was offered a job at the University of Hawaii in the beautiful Manoa Valley, just outside of Honolulu.

After high school she took some time off and worked at a number of odd jobs until she got "island fever" and left for Seattle to visit friends.

"I was walking downtown and heard someone say my name. I turned around and it was a former co-worker who was working in a frame shop. She told me they were hiring so I got my first job there. I never really planned on moving. It just kind of worked out and Seattle turned out to be a great place to live."

Now settled in Seattle, Lauren decided to enroll at Seattle Central Community College in 2000 and a few years later transferred to the University of Washington, where she graduated in 2004 with a B.S. in neuroscience.

School, though, was not all studying and no play. She began a romance with her future husband, Jason. She met him in 2001 through a friend who worked at the same hospital as Jason. The two were married in 2004 after Lauren received her diploma from the University of Washington.

"When I graduated, biotech was a very hot industry, so I got my first job with Amgen in Seattle. I worked for them for a couple of years and then moved to a very small start-up biotech company just as the bottom fell out of the market in 2008."

Luckily, Jason had been working with an employment recruiter for an information technology job in Switzerland, but that job turned out to be not a good fit for him. A second opportunity in Sydney, Australia, though, was. Even better, the company was American and Jason already knew some of the people who worked there.

"Neither of us had ever been to Sydney or Australia on vacation and had not even considered it because it was so far away. But when we asked some of our friends about moving to Sydney, they all said they would move to Australia 'in a heartbeat,' which gave us a little more confidence. It was a little weird moving to a place we had never been, but it turned out to be really great."

Once the decision to move was made, Lauren began searching on-line employment sites in Australia for job opportunities in the science research industry, and then applied directly to each company that had openings. She found a job in Sydney with Garvan Medical Research and was hired 'sight unseen' after a phone interview with her new manager.

She was fortunate that the hiring manager knew her former boss in Seattle through industry conferences. Her former employer had given her a very good recommendation.

Jason was the first employee his new company had recruited from abroad. He was given a cash stipend to cover their moving costs, visa expense and two weeks in a hotel upon arrival while they waited for their temporary work visas to be approved and looked for an apartment.

"Usually when you move somewhere in the U.S. you rent a U-Haul truck and bribe some friends with pizza and beer to help you. But moving nearly eight thousand miles across the world required a whole lot more planning. I searched online for international moving companies that served Australia and also asked for moving company recommendations from expats on various online forums. I finally decided on a local Seattle company. They had a good reputation and also shipped household goods worldwide through a network of affiliates. Interestingly, price turned out to not be the key factor. Most of the companies that we received bids from were pretty much the same. The differentiating factors for us were service, guarantees and the company's experience in international shipping."

Before the move, Lauren did her homework, searching a number of expat websites and online forums for information and answers to her questions. Her best source, though, turned out to be an older book she found while searching on Amazon called, *Americans' Survival Guide to Australia*. It became her indispensable companion as she prepared for their Australian adventure.

Their first two hectic weeks in Sydney were spent in a hotel while they waited for their temporary work permits to be approved by the government and looked for an apartment, which turned out to be a real challenge for the couple.

"We found that the real estate market in Sydney for renters was incredibly competitive. At first, we did not have any idea of how to go about it. We started going to apartment viewings and discovered that people were offering to pay higher rent, pay cash or pay a year in advance. We were in shock."

Lauren also did not realize that rental listings in Australia were based on price per week and not per month, believing at first that six hundred and fifty Australian dollars for a two-bedroom apartment was a steal. With the clock ticking, Lauren needed a strategy.

"I got online and realized there were only five major rental companies in Sydney and each company had a specific agent for each area of the city. We figured out where we wanted to live and then I started emailing those agents. I must have made a connection because some of them began responding to me and started tipping us off to available apartments before the listing was advertised."

They found a one-bedroom place in Elizabeth Bay, a harbor-side area just east of downtown Sydney, which was snug compared with their roomy three-bedroom duplex in Seattle. Their place back home also was half the cost. It was, though, just a ten-minute train ride from Jason's new job in Sydney's city center.

But after one year, their landlord informed them that their rent was going to go up one hundred Australian dollars a week. They were on the move again, sooner than they had planned, landing this time in a residential area north of Sydney harbor called Neutral Bay.

"Neutral Bay was more of a suburban neighborhood and right on Sydney harbor. It was quiet there. I had not realized the noise of the city and the change was nice. We had a view of Sydney and the opera house, and a little park just down the way. With all the trees and parks in the area, birds seemed to be everywhere. One of the birds was the Kookaburra, which started its very loud laugh about a half hour before sunrise. At first I thought it was a monkey. That bird drove me crazy."

After three years of working for her new company in Sydney, Lauren lost her job when funding for the project she was working on ran out. But soon after moving to Australia, she had started an expat blog about daily life in the country, reporting on differences in Australian coffee and the coffee back home and other similar topics. Now unemployed, she decided it was time to turn her blog into a real business.

"I started getting a lot of emails from readers asking me specific questions about moving to Australia, so I said to myself: 'I need to start writing about this.' I remembered when I moved here how difficult it was combing through all of the websites just to find out specific information about Sydney. My first blog was more of a travel journal, but the new blog I created, sydneymovingguide.com, was more nuts and bolts about moving to Sydney and what to expect. People liked it because it was all about Sydney and Australia and they were hungry for first-hand information."

Her first blog was called "emeraldcitytoaus.com," a reference to one of Seattle's nicknames, but she soon discovered that Sydney also was once called the emerald city and began searching for a domain name that would better communicate what the blog was about. When she changed her domain name to sydneymovingguide.com, a name that better described what the blog provided, the number of visitors began to skyrocket.

The fast-growing growing blog also found appeal among advertisers interested in Lauren's niche audience, and revenue started pouring in.

With new income from Lauren's business, the couple moved for the third time in 2012 to their current home in Woolahra, close to Sydney's famous Bondi Beach. The posh area has many historic houses and is just fifteen minutes by train to Jason's work in the center of Sydney.

"We live in a two-bedroom apartment in a small six-unit building on a ridge that provides us with a bit of a view of Sydney harbor. We also love that Bondi Beach is just five minutes by car or an easy half-hour walk."

As city dwellers, one of the things Lauren and Jason love about Sydney is its transportation system, which is much better than Seattle's. Providing multiple forms of transportation, including an extensive rail system, it takes them wherever they want to go quickly and cheaply.

Although commuting to work and getting around the city is a breeze for them, the couple decided to buy a car several years ago, mainly for long road trips.

"Every chance we get we take a long weekend, a camping trip or an extended vacation. There are just so many places to see in Australia because it is so vast and varied. One of our first big trips was to the Australia Open in Melbourne. We drove from Sydney to Melbourne along the coast, which took us about two weeks because we stopped at all of the little beach towns along the way. My favorite was Jervis Bay, which is south of Sydney. It is a little bay that is home to a pod of dolphins and also whales, depending on the time of year you visit."

When they reached Melbourne, they discovered Mornington Peninsula, just southeast of Melbourne, surrounded by Port Philip Bay, Western Port and Bass Straight.

"It is kind of like Sonoma in California, a great wine area with plenty of beautiful beaches nearby. It is one of our favorite wine areas in Australia.

We love the Pinot Noir but the local wineries produce a wide variety, including, of course, Australia's famous Shiraz."

Another of Lauren's favorite spots is Port Douglas, over one thousand miles north of Queensland's capital, Brisbane. The laid-back coastal town offers diving and snorkeling tours of Australia's natural treasure, the Great Barrier Reef.

Back in the city, Lauren and Jason developed a new network of friends, who helped them integrate into their new life abroad. But so far, the majority of their friends have been expats, including Australians who moved abroad as expats and returned home.

"We often use meetup.com to get together with other Americans in Sydney, mostly active, younger expats. We do things like going out Friday nights for drinks, watching NFL games together and things like that. When you move to a new place, particularly a foreign country, it takes a while to establish relationships. We felt very isolated at first, so we looked for other expats because they share the same interests and challenges as you."

Culture shock also is a common occurrence for new expats. For Lauren, it was discovering how patriotic she really was when faced with Australian misperceptions of America.

"We know that the people in the television series *Jersey Shore* and other U.S. reality shows do not represent America, but many Australians do not. I spent a lot of time trying to correct these misperceptions about Americans and how we live and what we stand for. All Americans do not walk around with a gun strapped to their waist, as many Australians believe. Another thing I had to explain to my Australian friends was our system of government and our voting procedures, which they really do not understand. Here, they have a parliamentary system and, by law, all Australians must vote. I have learned that living abroad gives you a whole different perspective on the United States."

Lauren also has learned that one of the benefits of living in Australia is excellent healthcare for all at a very reasonable price. If they were permanent residents of the country, they would qualify for the Australian healthcare system, which underwrites most healthcare costs for those who qualify. But with renewable temporary work visas, they must buy private insurance, which costs them a reasonable two hundred and fifty Australian dollars each month for full coverage.

"Another great thing we have found about living in Australia is Superannuation, which is a government-supported program that requires our employers to pay a proportion of our salaries and wages into a superannuation fund. It is currently about nine and a half percent of our wages but will go up to twelve percent over the next few years. People are also encouraged to put aside additional funds into superannuation. That additional 'nest egg' really helps because the Sydney cost of living is very high, especially rents."

But even with a higher cost of living in Sydney, Lauren and Jason love living in the city for its lifestyle and culture.

"We have the wonderful Sydney opera house, so there is always something going on there like a play, a symphony or a concert. During our winter, they light the opera house for the annual light festival, which makes it so beautiful at night. Then there is the noodle market in Hyde Park, where all the Asian restaurants have food stalls. It is great fun with great food and they decorate the park with Chinese lanterns, as well. Sculptures by the Sea, a public art show that stretches from Bondi beach to Bronte beach, is another favorite of ours. Every month something is happening in Sydney."

Lauren thinks one of the best decisions they made when they first moved to the city was to buy season tickets for the Sydney Theater Company, which they attend every month.

When at home, the couple cozies up to watch Australian television, which carries not only local programs, but also American and British shows. They do not have either satellite or cable television service but rather rely on DVDs to binge watch a whole season of shows, like HBO's *Game of Thrones.*

Now that they are completely settled and flourishing in Sydney, Lauren is giving some thought to going back to school for her Ph.D.

"If I was an Australian citizen and going for my doctoral degree, the government would actually pay me to go back to school. A lot of the Ph.D.s I worked with got their education this way. It is great because they do not have to go into debt to advance their education and the country needs well-educated workers."

But she is not an Australian citizen and would have to pay the full costs of the two-year Ph.D. program, although it would still be far less expensive than a comparable program in the United States. She is still mulling it over.

Like most expats, one of the biggest disadvantages of living in the land down under is the separation from family and friends. Although she stays in touch through Skype, Facebook and other social media, she worries that she still may lose touch with those she loves.

"When we first moved to Sydney we returned home several times a year but that has now tapered off to once every several years. And, unfortunately, many of our friends who were hit hard by the 2008 recession still have not gotten back on their feet financially and cannot afford to visit us."

One of the things the couple still has not completely adjusted to after six years of living in Sydney is the Australian take on the English language.

"Sometimes it is hard to believe that we speak the same language. For example, one of my co-workers was going away on holiday and I was taking over her project. She told me, 'I usually come over here and take a quick squiz.' I said, 'You take a what?' She said, 'Oh, it means a quick look.' People say they will take a quick squiz at the menu in a restaurant. I guess it would be the same for expats in the States getting used to our slang words."

Now that Lauren and Jason have mostly decoded the language they plan to stay a while. They are on their first renewal of the four-year temporary work visas they received when they entered the country.

"The question now is: Do we become permanent residents? If we do, are we after Australian citizenship? Should we think about putting down roots in Sydney? We have actually been talking about moving to the U.K., and France was even in the discussion at one point. You know, once you get bit by the expat bug, you become an expat forever."

CHAPTER 11

Whelma Cabanawan
Age 30
Budapest, Hungary

"I think a part of me never thought it was possible to leave Los Angeles. I never thought it was possible to live in another country, to actually be here in Hungary. I am not going to say I have traveled the world because I have not. But I am getting there."

WHELMA CABANAWAN DREAMED of traveling the world, but she could never find the time to get away from her demanding job in Los Angeles. That all changed in 2012 when an unexpected death sent her on a journey to heal her soul and find a new adventure in Budapest, Hungary.

Born in a rural village four hours from Manilla, Whelma lived the first ten years of her life in the Philippines. Her dad worked for the Ferdinand Marcos regime in the government's agriculture department before that country's revolution in the nineteen-eighties. He later founded his own company, selling fertilizers and chemicals to farmers. Her mother was a nurse who left the family to work in Oman when Whelma was just six months old.

Her parents decided to immigrate to the United States in 1992, settling in New Jersey where her mom, who was fluent in English, went to work as a nurse. Her prideful father could not speak English and had to start as a janitor.

Finally secure in their new life in New Jersey, Whelma's parents sent for their children to join them in America.

"I remember specifically that it was 1993 because the worst blizzard in New Jersey's history happened that year. It was the first time we had ever seen snow and it was a little weird."

Three years later the family decided to escape the cold northeastern winters and move south to join family in the more benign climate of Jacksonville, Florida.

"Going to New Jersey was a culture shock for me when I was just ten years old, but I think Jacksonville was even worse. I think my mom may have been trying play with our minds. She brought us from one of the most diverse places in America to a city that was not diverse at all."

After graduating from high school in Jacksonville, Whelma chose the University of Central Florida in Orlando for her college education, which was less than a three-hour drive away. She majored in political science with an eye to becoming an attorney.

"My plan was to go to law school but during my senior year I ended up visiting my best friend, who had moved from Jacksonville to Los Angeles. He was going to UCLA and interning with a non-profit organization. I ended up volunteering for the same organization and took a year off from UCF to get really engaged in the immigrant rights movement. "

After joining thousands of others on May 1, 2006 to march for immigrant rights in Los Angeles, Whelma made a career decision to spend the rest of her life working for the rights of others.

Following graduation from the University of Central Florida in 2007, she headed back to Los Angeles and landed a job with the Coalition for

Humane Immigrant Rights Los Angeles (CHIRLA), where she had interned for a semester during her senior year at school.

It was the right career choice for Whelma. She was passionate about her work and wanted to succeed, and for her that meant advancing her education. She found a MBA program at the American Jewish University in L.A. that was tailored for non-profit organization management. The school awarded her a scholarship and CHIRLA provided additional education assistance money to help her attend. After working full-time and attending school full-time, Whelma graduated with her master's degree in 2009.

But it was not all "nose to the grindstone" for Whelma. She began dating Jose, who was a community organizer for one of CHIRLA's sister organizations. After dating for a few years, the couple decided to buy a house together and get married. But that was not to be.

Jose was killed in a snowboarding accident in March of 2012.

"He was just twenty-seven years old and it just really shook me. I loved him so much and we had made so many plans for the future. After the funeral, I left my house, my job and everything. I was in complete shock. I had to take a bereavement leave for a month and get away. My dad took me back to the Philippines to begin my healing process."

She had not been back to her family home in the Philippines for twenty years. Seeing her grandparents and new family that had been born since she left was just what she needed.

"It is still really something to go back to the land where you were born. When I arrived I felt very connected. It really helped me with my grieving process to go to a place where Jose had never been. I saw him everywhere."

After returning to work, Whelma found that traveling helped her heal and from that point forward made it a personal goal to go somewhere new every month, even if it was just in California.

"Before, I never had the time to really travel because I was doing civil rights work, which is very demanding. I was working all of the time because we were a grass roots organization and the work just had to get done. But Jose's death changed everything for me."

She tried to concentrate on her work and live alone in the home she and Jose shared, but her life had changed completely.

"After six months, I decided I needed to leave L.A. for my peace of mind. I regretted that I had not traveled more, that I had not experienced life in another country. That is when I set my goal to live somewhere else in the world."

She had worked for CHIRLA for seven long, hard years and knew she was not going to replace her executive director anytime soon. It was a perfect time to change her life.

"I started thinking about the best way for me to accomplish my goal, to live somewhere else and travel. For me, the best way to get there was to go back to school. I knew that getting more education would not hurt me and would probably make me more attractive to potential employers, particularly if the additional education included study abroad. I started filling out college applications, looking for a scholarship that would help fund my education and allow me to live in another country."

Not waiting to hear back from the schools she had applied to, Whelma rented her house to a friend to cover her monthly mortgage expense and boarded a plane to the Philippines for a six-month stay. She had saved money from her job with CHIRLA, so financially she was fine.

"When I was in the Philippines this time I volunteered with an international relief organization that was providing assistance to the victims of a major typhoon. While I was there, I lived in the house I grew up in and spent most of my time helping those who were hit hardest by the storm."

After working long, hard hours helping others, Whelma finally took some much needed time off to visit Indonesia, Malaysia, Cambodia and Dubai to help restore her depleted energy.

While still in the Philippines, she began receiving acceptance letters from the schools she had applied to earlier. She specifically was looking for a program that would allow her to live abroad. Whelma found it at St. John's University in New York.

"They had a two-year social justice program in global development that allowed me to spend summers in Rome. I thought that was perfect. I could live in Rome, study and travel, and they were giving me a forty percent scholarship."

She left for Rome in the summer of 2014 to begin her studies. While in Rome, she received an email from Central European University in Budapest, Hungary that upended her plan to study at St. John's.

"I was on the waiting list for Central European University because they only accept twelve students for each program. I was excited because it was an eighty percent scholarship and the tuition was a lot lower than I was paying at St. John's. It was a master's program in human rights, something I had always wanted. I ended up withdrawing from St. John's and spending the rest of the summer traveling to Paris, Brussels, Venice, Istanbul and other cities I had only read about it."

Before arriving in Budapest, Whelma did more research on her new school and learned that George Soros, the global philanthropist and

Budapest native, founded Central European University in 1991. It was a graduate-level-only English-language school attended by more than fifteen hundred students from one hundred countries and was one of the wealthiest universities in Europe, with an endowment of nearly one billion dollars.

"I found that the school had incredible diversity, attracting students from all over the world, particularly from developing and third world countries. Graduates return to their countries and become leaders. Giorgi Margvelashvili, the President of Georgia, was a graduate of the school."

When Whelma arrived in Budapest she could see the vestiges of Hungary's occupation by the Soviet Union, not only the buildings and architecture, but also the conservative, cautious attitudes and behavior of the formerly suppressed Hungarian people.

Whelma quickly learned that one of the keys to a smooth cultural integration in a new country is to learn the language. Her school was English-speaking, but she still had to live her everyday life among people who communicated in one of the world's most difficult languages.

"The Hungarian language is really difficult. I have learned to say, 'Hi, hello, thank you' and a few other basic words and phrases. My mom asks if I am learning the language and I tell her the names of the train stations, which she thinks is good. Being in a community of international students helps, but at the same time it does not force me to learn the language because we all speak English."

The university is ideally located just a block from Saint Stephen's Basilica in Budapest's main square and is just a short walk from Whelma's one-bedroom apartment in the city center.

"After I arrived I began losing hope in finding a really good apartment. I decided not to look online before I came because I was told by the apartment search office at the school to avoid online apartment searching because of all the scams that were going on. I was able to find an apartment after I began my classes, and I love it."

Budapest housing is very inexpensive, certainly relative to high-priced California, her former home. Whelma's apartment has a full bedroom with a king-sized bed, a full bath and a large kitchen. She loves that it is on the fourth floor of a courtyard apartment building, which provides her with a nice view of the spacious courtyard below.

"In L.A., my apartment would easily rent for about fifteen hundred dollars a month but I pay just three hundred eighty dollars a month, not including electricity, which runs another one hundred dollars a month during the winter. Plus, the apartment is located in a very safe neighborhood only three-minutes from my school."

Whelma's apartment building is over one hundred years old. She found it through a class she was taking on archives and human rights because of the building's historical significance. In Budapest, buildings inhabited by Jews during World War II were marked with a yellow star. Her building was one of the buildings the people of Hungary commemorate.

Living in the heart of Budapest provides Whelma with a wide range of restaurants close at hand. She rarely eats out, though, because so many of them in the city center cater primarily to tourists and are quite expensive relative to other places to eat in the city.

"In Budapest, we have a joke: 'If the menu outside is in Euros, it is either not good or it caters primarily to tourists.' I think Hungarian food is good but it still resembles the heavy food served during the days of the Soviets: lots of bad meat, potatoes, salt and a lot of seasoning to make it taste good. Since I have my own kitchen, I cook a lot for myself and friends."

Most of her friends are fellow students at the university. Many of them, as with previous students who attended her university, intend to remain in Budapest. She has met some who have been working in the city for three to five years, mainly because they find it cheaper to live in Budapest than other European cities and it is centrally located for travel throughout the continent.

"One of my goals when I moved here was to be in a different country each month. I just came back from Vienna, which is just two and a half hours away by bus. I love Vienna because there is so much to see and do and, by the way, the weather is a lot better."

Weather is a concern for Whelma, who loved the warm weather climates of California, Florida and the Philippines. It gets cold and dark by mid-afternoon in Budapest during the winter, which makes her despondent and sometimes affects her attitude.

Although Budapest's climate affects her mood, she still thinks it is a great place to live, particularly the history and culture the city offers.

"I try to visit something new at least once a week. Recently, I visited the Shoes on the Danube Bank memorial, which was created to honor the Jews who were killed during World War II. I do the same thing when I travel to Vienna. I visit a new museum each day I am there. I loved seeing the Monet collection at one of my favorite art museums there."

Whelma also was happy to find that her school is an oasis of cultural diversity, even though Budapest, she believes, is not.

"In my program alone there are students from over thirty-five countries. I am around different people from different backgrounds all day long, but when I leave school it is a lot different. Coming from Los Angeles, which is very multicultural, I found that living in a much more homogenous city and country is a very different experience. Sometimes I encounter people who do not like the fact that we expats are living in Budapest. I think it would probably help if I spoke at least some Hungarian to get to know them better."

Few older Hungarians speak English but younger people study English in school, usually beginning in grade school. Many in Budapest, both young and old, are concerned that the city is catering more and more to tourists and an influx of expats.

"One of my friends who lives here was telling me one day after school that she recently checked out a bar that she knew had cheap drinks. But when she got there, she discovered that the inexpensive bar had been replaced by what she called a 'hipster' bar, which now caters primarily to expats. She really hated the idea that Budapest is changing. She said told me that Budapest ten years ago looked a lot different than it does today."

To widen her social contacts and get her out of her apartment more often, Whelma went online and signed up for a local expat Budapest Facebook group, which meets every Tuesday for drinks and socializing.

"It is very cool because I think sometimes it is nice to just be around folks that get me and have some of the same complaints and needs that I do. One of the things we all seem to agree on is service here in Budapest. There definitely is a lack of customer service here. In the States, everybody tips for the most part, but here a lot of people do not leave tips. So servers tend to not really care about the type of service they give you."

She also has been having a hard time getting used to the reserve of the Hungarian people and those from other Central and Eastern European countries.

"It is not that they are cold, it is just that the culture here is so very different from ours. I am from California and I am a Filipina. We are very happy-go-lucky, outgoing people. I always want to laugh and be happy. My outlook on life is very different from the people around me. It makes it doubly difficult when you do not have any family or friends around."

Whelma does love the European approach to life, though. She admires and embraces a more leisurely pace where people take their time to eat and drink and often just sit at a coffeehouse to spend time with others and socialize.

Although she loves the more leisurely approach to life, her ambition continues to drive her forward. Before graduation, she will do research for her thesis at the libraries of the United Nations and International Labor Organization (ILO) in Geneva, Switzerland.

"I am doing my thesis on an International Labor Organization treaty that was passed in 2012, giving rights to domestic workers all over the world. I received a grant from the ILO to do the work. It is going to be really interesting because I got approved to do it under the ILO's civil disobedience department."

Whelma also was selected to be a civil disobedience intern at the Hungarian Civil Liberties Union.

Her interest and education in international human rights work will dictate the path Whelma takes in the near future. Her experience has taught her that she can do almost anything she wants, once she determines what that "anything" is.

"I do not think I will be living in Hungary after I graduate. It is really too conservative for me. What I do really depends on my experience working with the International Labor Organization. I can definitely see myself living in Vienna, particularly because the United Nations and a number of other big international associations have offices there. I also love the fact that Vienna is a very diverse city and has a Philippine community. That could be a real clincher for me. "

CHAPTER 12

Greg Webb
Age 25
Cologne, Germany

"I was thinking of spending just a year abroad, but once I got there things changed. When you finally get to live in another culture it gives you a totally different perspective from your own country. It really flips your ideas upside down."

ALTHOUGH GREG WEBB was the child of a career soldier, he never had the chance to live abroad. But when a serious chronic medical disorder derailed his dream of working in law enforcement, he set off on an adventure to Germany that changed his world.

Greg was born in Philadelphia and raised in the small town of Tabernacle, New Jersey, just fifteen minutes from Atlantic City. His mom was a nurse practitioner and dad was a career soldier who spent twenty years serving his country, both home and abroad. Although stationed overseas twice in his career, he never took his family with him when he was assigned to bases in other countries.

After high school, Greg decided to follow in his father's footsteps and joined the army, spending the next four years in South Carolina and Arizona as an intelligence analyst.

Like many young, small town Americans, Greg's motivation to serve had much to do with the education benefits provided by the U.S.

government. After his service ended in 2010, he enrolled at Purdue University in Lafayette, Indiana, but left after just one semester, not yet ready to tackle the rigors of a major university.

Greg had served his basic training in South Carolina and liked the southern state. After the misfire at Purdue, he recalibrated his career aspirations by attending Trident Technical College, a two-year school located in North Charleston.

"I guess I was not ready for Purdue, so I left after just one semester to get my bearings. Trident had a very good criminal justice program, which I was very interested in as a possible career."

He graduated from Trident with an Associate of Applied Science degree in 2012 and set his sights on a career in law enforcement or corrections, but that all changed when he was diagnosed with epilepsy.

"Throughout my life I had focal seizures, which pretty much went undiagnosed. Then, when I was around twenty-two, it started getting really bad. The doctors continued to tell me that my symptoms indicated hypoglycemia. They said that I needed to have a more consistent eating schedule. When it was finally properly diagnosed, all of my plans went out the window. It is very hard to get into any police academy with epilepsy."

The realization that he would not be able to pursue a law enforcement career struck Greg hard. He began to think about what he could do with his life that would be interesting and accommodate his medical condition.

"I was quite discouraged for a while until I heard from a friend of mine who was working at Google in Ireland and thought there might be an opportunity for me there. I was ready for a change, a new adventure. Unfortunately, that connection did not pan out for me but it got me thinking about the possibilities of living and working in Europe. I started looking for a job in other European countries."

Greg conducted extensive online research to find a job that would meet his very specific needs. He found a wide range of opportunities with companies that provided European clients with English translation services, particularly for online activities like social media and search.

"I was applying primarily in Ireland, England, Spain and Germany and sent out a curriculum vitae for about fifty English-translation jobs in those countries. It took about three or four months before I heard from anyone. I used primarily online recruiters in my search, which I highly recommend. A particularly good one was MGI Recruitment, which specializes in language placements. They are very, very good at placing people and keeping you in their system for new opportunities."

Through MGI, Greg heard from Appen, a global company with an office in Berlin, Germany. Appen provides speech and search technology services for mainly information technology companies.

"They are a worldwide company with translators that speak around one hundred and fifty different languages. Appen provides consulting services, legal document translation and things like that. They contacted me to do basic web search evaluation, like correcting Google errors and working on social media usage where knowing English is important. They were looking for native English-speakers who would know how to frame Google questions for German clients."

Before Greg was hired as a web search evaluator for Appen, he had to take a series of tests to determine his proficiency with search engines and English, and demonstrate the mastery of other technical skills that would be required in his new position.

He accepted Appen's offer to work for them as a contract employee in July of 2013 and began preparation for his move to Germany, which included some online research, but not nearly enough.

"I wish I had spent more time finding out about Germany. I also would advise anyone thinking about moving abroad to not make a quick decision. Moving abroad is a big deal and should not be taken lightly. Definitely take the time to put a plan together, maybe a year in advance. Social media is a great way to reach out to people who live there and find out what it is like to live in the country and what you need to know. You need to get your ducks in a row so you can deal with things that often just come out of left field. One thing, for sure, is to save as much money as you can before you move."

Greg left Charleston a month after signing his contract with Appen, shoving a few things into his old army-issued duffle bag and boarding a plane for Frankfurt.

"After I touched down in Frankfurt and stepped outside of the airport, the realization of being in Germany just hit me like a cloudburst. I was in a foreign land, jet-lagged and exhausted. But at the same time, I was also excited and could not wait to get to my new home"

Greg's new contract job with Appen allowed him to work remotely anywhere in the country. He decided to begin his new life in Germany in Marburg, a vibrant university town of less than one hundred thousand people, about an hour's drive north of Frankfurt. His plan was to work and take a few classes at the University of Marburg, which would help him integrate into the German culture.

Marburg was a good choice for him since one-quarter of the city's population attends the university, an easy adjustment for Greg who had just graduated from a two-year school. He enrolled in a German class and a sports class for the fall semester while working a thirty-five hour week. Greg used his time at the university to familiarize himself with the German language and culture, explore the surrounding countryside and cities and begin friendships with students he met from many other countries.

"I especially liked the nightlife in Marburg but it was a lot different from what I was used to back home. My friends and I used to go out around nine or ten at night and party until around two in the morning. In Marburg, everyone would meet at an apartment to start drinking and then would not go out until around midnight. The partying usually continued until about six. That was pretty hard to get used to, but I got used to it."

Although Greg had studied German in high school, he quickly learned that it was not enough for any kind of conversation. Since he was working in the language translation business and wanted a full and active social life, he knew it was important to get up to speed on the language as quickly as he could. He had a problem, though. Many Germans wanted to practice their English skills with him, not speak German.

The university's German language class helped Greg reach the B1 level of language competency, which placed him in the middle of the A1 to C2 seven-point scale of competence. Level C2 represents complete fluency. To qualify for a German visa, level A1 competence is required.

"Most of the German teachers I have spoken with have told me that going from my present level of B1 to C2 is the really hard part. Right now I am at the strong conversational level, but reaching C2 is my goal."

Before the fall semester ended, Greg decided to move to Germany's fourth largest city, Cologne, which spreads along the banks of the Rhine River in west-central Germany.

"I had a friend who moved to Cologne and really liked it. He was constantly Skyping me when I was living in Marburg, sending me photos of the city and the surrounding area. One weekend I decided to go there to see a concert with him and I instantly fell in love with the city. Since I was not tied to living in any particular place, I thought why not move to Cologne. It was a little hard to leave Marburg, though, because I had started dating a German girl that I liked a lot. "

Before he moved to Cologne, Greg found an apartment by looking online for a shared flat to reduce expenses. In Germany, a shared flat is called a WG and is commonly used by students and young people who are concerned about living costs.

"I started searching for a WG roommate on Facebook, but you can also just Google WG to find lots of availabilities all over Germany. I searched for about six weeks before I found a place to live because it is difficult to find a reasonably priced place to rent in Cologne."

With an hourly salary of fifteen dollars, Greg could not afford to live in the city center, so he opted for a shared flat in Bruehl, a village about fifteen minutes from Cologne's magnificent cathedral. He splits the monthly rent with a young German man about his age.

"Because housing is hard to find in Cologne, and expensive, living outside the city is much easier for me and a lot cheaper. I do not have to commute to an office, which also means I do not need a car, which is expensive to own and operate in Germany. I discovered that public transportation is very convenient and well priced, so I take trains and buses everywhere."

Greg often takes a bus from Cologne to Marburg to visit his German girlfriend, who is studying English at the university. He prefers it to the train because he does not have to change trains and German buses are much more inexpensive.

"The bus ride to Marburg takes about two and a half hours and is very comfortable. The bus is equipped with Wi-Fi, a spotless bathroom and serves refreshments along the way. It only costs a little over ten dollars one-way, so I can visit her about three times a month. I do a lot of work on the bus with my laptop, which is a real plus. Trains are getting a lot more expensive, so I wonder why more people are not taking the bus?"

Greg has found a large expat community living in Cologne through both social media and the local club scene and has become close friends with several expats, not all Americans. Two of his closest friends, an Italian and a German, just moved from Cologne, but his social contacts continue to expand.

"Social meet-ups are big in Germany, especially through something called couch surfing. There are websites where you can write a message asking people throughout the country if you can sleep on their couch for a night or two. It is cool because it is free and you get to see reviews based on each person's couch surfing experience. There are a lot of couch surfing groups and it is a great way for people from other countries to get connected, although it is still mainly for young people."

Besides his search evaluation work for Appen, Greg now also handles some crowd-sourcing projects and social media assignments for other clients who want to use social media to market to an English-speaking audience.

"When a client posts something on their Facebook group page, they want to make sure that it can go as viral as possible so that it calls attention to their post. We are constantly trying to improve their results. I try to find common words within the post that will attract more people to generate the most traffic for our client."

This new work has expanded Greg's attractiveness to other project managers from within the company. They frequently contact him for additional assignments in other countries. As a freelance contractor, he can accept other work from within the company, if he has the time.

"Two or three months ago a project manager from Australia contacted me and asked if I could translate a document from German to English. That, however, was a bit out of my competence area since I am still learning German. But I like the fact that the company has a worldwide database that allows other project managers to contact me for jobs that will add to my earnings."

Greg's contract with Appen is for a year at a time, subject to a performance review. So far, his reviews have been good. He likes his job but there are a few downsides. When he first arrived in Germany, the company handled all of the paperwork for his work permit visa, which also includes temporary residency status in Germany. But as a temporary resident and a contract employee, his healthcare needs are not covered under Germany's national plan

"I have to pay for my own health insurance out-of-pocket, which is difficult because of my epilepsy. I had a pretty bad episode while I was living in Marburg. Since I was in the middle of transitioning my health insurance coverage at the time, it left me with a pretty big bill. Fortunately, I have been able to pay it off."

Besides the cost of private health insurance, Greg is also concerned about the over forty percent German tax bite, which is much higher than the U.S. On the other hand, his daily cost of living expenses in Germany are much more affordable than he thought.

"The transportation system here is so good and inexpensive that you really do not need a car, which really helps with my daily living expenses. The cost of gas alone does not justify owning a car. I am finding that food also is less expensive. My food bill runs less than thirty dollars a week, which is less than I paid back home."

Greg has settled in for the long-term in Germany and thinks that the job he found with Appen may be a great way for other Millennials to live in another country and earn a living.

"People say that my age group is the first digital generation because we have grown up online. A lot of companies are looking for people like us who speak English and are Internet savvy. With all of the online recruiters, it is pretty easy to find a job. Once you are hired, the company takes care of everything. I especially like what I am doing because I can work anywhere, and I am pretty sure that is attractive to lots of others like me."

Greg will remain in Germany and continue working for Appen, but he also has applied to Schiller International University, a private school with campuses in Largo, Florida; Heidelberg, Germany; Paris, France; and Madrid, Spain.

He will move to Heidelberg in the fall to enroll in the international relations program and hopefully get his bachelor's degree in a few years. Greg especially likes the idea that the school also will allow him to take a semester in Paris or Madrid. The curriculum structure at the school is just one class per month, instead of the usual four or five classes for a full semester, which will help Greg fit his classes into his work schedule.

"I think this will work out well because I love Germany, my job is going great and I want to stay here. When I lived in the States I used to think it would be good to travel to gain some cultural perspective, but I was not really thinking about actually living in another country. Now that I am here, I am really glad that I made the move."

Nicky Bryce-Sharron
Age 29
Brighton, England

"Moving to Brighton was sort of like the official start of my adult life. I moved here, got married and found a real job. From now on I could be whoever I wanted to be. It was the start of a new beginning."

MILFORD, OHIO IS a conservative, sleepy little town of about seven thousand people just northeast of Cincinnati. It was the kind of town young liberal men and women wanted to leave as soon as they finished high school.

Nicky Bryce-Sharron was one of those young people. She left Milford in her rear view mirror when she was eighteen and moved to Lake Charles, Louisiana to attend McNeese State University, aiming for a double major in psychology and sociology. But Hurricanes Rita and Katrina gave Lake Charles a one-two punch and knocked Nicky and her roommate out of their apartment after her first two years in school. She never returned.

Nicky had an ordinary small town America childhood, growing up with her two younger brothers. Dad was an operating room nurse for years until he retired. Mom managed the office for the local American Lung Association. Family trips during her childhood never left the shores of America.

She returned home to Milford after the hurricanes ended her immediate school plans and took a local retail job to earn her keep. Her real interest, though, was online, where she could find the adventure missing in her life amidst the electrons connecting her with like-minded people from all over the world.

"In the evening after work I started playing World of Warcraft, which was a massively multiplayer online role-playing game. That is where I met my future husband, Mark. He also loved online gaming. We were in the same guild, or player organization. Mark and I communicated through voice commands and voice programs, like Skype. We started talking and pretty soon game talk became personal talk, and eventually we just met up."

Mark, who is seven years older than Nicky, lived in Brighton, England, the famous seaside resort city on the south coast, about forty minutes by train from London.

"We met online in the summer of 2006 and had a long-distance relationship for about a year and a half. I visited Mark in Brighton several times before I moved over there, which was the first time in my life I had ever left the U.S. We got married in Milford in October of 2007 but it took about another three months before the visa paperwork came through and I could legally join Mark in Brighton."

The United Kingdom does not grant automatic citizenship to spouses of U.K. citizens, so Nicky remains in England on a United Kingdom Permanent Residence visa. The visa provides an "Indefinite leave to remain," which allows her to work or start a business there and has no time limits on her stay in the United Kingdom. Nicky plans to apply for citizenship this year.

After setting up their new home in a rented apartment in Brighton, Nicky set about finding a new job and landed one at the local American

Express office with the help of Mark, who had worked for the company for several years in customer service.

"It was the first real, adult job I ever had. I worked for American Express in their customer service department for about five years, but we both knew that we wanted something of our own, something that could be built on what we love and what we are really good at: the Internet."

Nicky and Mark launched their new business, called Sussex SEO, not long after she started working with Mark at American Express. Their company develops websites for primarily local small businesses and promotes them through search engine optimization (SEO) marketing, which helps their clients rank higher in Google search engine rankings.

"It was very difficult for the first few years because we both were essentially working two full-time jobs. And then in 2010, I gave birth to our daughter, Madeline. That actually helped somewhat because I was able to take a leave of absence for a year to care for the baby and had more time to focus on my education."

While working at American Express, starting a new business and having a baby, super mom Nicky also enrolled at Open University, a public research university, and one of the biggest universities in the UK for undergraduate education.

"It is mostly online course work but you do meet up with your class to have localized study groups once in awhile. End of year exams also are done offline in a classroom. Since I am studying for a biology degree, my lab work is also done in a classroom. Most of the offline classes are held at Sussex or Brighton Universities."

Nicky's university program is a three-year degree. It will take her several more years to finish because they did not accept her U.S. credits for transfer and she can only study part-time. Mark also attends Open University and will receive his degree in a few years as well.

Finally tiring of the hours they were putting in juggling school, their jobs and their new business, and with a rush of new business customers developed by Mark, the couple decided to leave their jobs at American Express and incorporate Sussex SEO in 2013.

"By the time we incorporated our company we had developed enough business to sustain our lifestyle without our full-time jobs at American Express. Not having to work two jobs each was a big relief for us, especially with a young child at home."

Many of their Sussex county and Brighton clients are in trade skills, like plumbing and electrical work, and most are local, but they do have a customer in France, one in Spain and several in the United States.

Although Nicky and Mark build websites for some of their clients, most of their income comes from SEO marketing expertise. Google search engine rankings are very important for small clients because it is their primary way of marketing to their customers.

Besides website creation and SEO marketing, Nicky and Mark also handle brand management for smaller clients who do not have the resources to do their own marketing. Larger clients usually have marketing resources and are just looking for SEO to push their brand up in the Google rankings for their business category.

"Almost all of our business has been generated by word of mouth. It is kind of funny that we are SEO experts but never have the time to do SEO for ourselves. We get good results, though, for our clients and that is why they recommend us."

Most of their clients turn into ongoing relationships, primarily because they are not only satisfied with the results they receive but are assured that Nicky and Mark also stay on the leading edge of online marketing techniques.

The business had grown substantially by the time the business was incorporated in 2013 and required additional helping hands to handle the work load.

"We needed help to keep up with the business. To hire employees, we had to convert from a sole proprietorship to a limited company. We could not do it ourselves so we hired a solicitor to help us through the process. Never try this on your own. We paid a professional to do it and it was very easy with no paperwork nightmares. It took just two months to get everything done."

The company expanded to include eight employees, six located in the Philippines and two in Brighton, who joined Nicky and Mark in a new office conveniently located just around the corner from the couple's flat.

"We bought a flat less than two blocks from the sea in Brighton. I absolutely love it here because it is just such a colorful place to live. Being a beautiful city and right on the sea, you get a lot of people from all over the world who are either settling, like myself, or just stopping in on their way somewhere else. Brighton is a very transient place. You get to meet people with a lot of very different views, especially in the summertime. There is no place like Brighton. Something is always going on here."

Their flat, a converted house with a basement, is in a family-oriented neighborhood about fifteen minutes outside of Brighton's city center and a leisurely stroll from the beach. The three-bedroom flat was needed for the expansion of their family with the arrival of their son, Dexter, last year.

"I am home for a while on maternity leave until Dexter is old enough for school. It also helps a lot that Madeline now attends a nearby private school most of the day. Between the kids, work and school and the usual household stuff, I have a pretty full day."

She still has time, though, to enjoy and engage with the people of Brighton, who Nicky has found to be quite different from the small town conservatives of her hometown in Ohio.

"I think Brighton and most of southeast England are just more liberal, more accepting of political and religious opinions. I love it because I consider myself a liberal atheist and that combination in Milford is not appreciated that much."

She feels much more free to express her views in Brighton and no longer fears being metaphorically "burned at the stake" for holding views counter to what she believes is the dogma of small town America.

Like most expats, Nicky spends a lot of time online using social media to connect with others who share her expatriate experiences. She has met a number of people who share her views and likes and dislikes.

"There are a number of Facebook groups for American expats in the U.K. The one I joined has over one thousand members, so it is very easy to meet quite a few people in your area. Most are in their late twenties or early thirties. I keep adding new friends and now our annual Thanksgiving dinner is up to eighteen people. I may have to get a bigger house."

Many of her American expat friends, like her, married British spouses, bought houses and started families. Brighton is an attractive place to live for many of them because commuting to work in London is just a matter of hopping on a train for forty minutes.

"I do not know that many other American expats who have started businesses here, except my closest friend, Jen. She is a self-employed free-lance writer who does copy editing and copywriting and is a novelist in her spare time. We use her services quite often."

Nicky has found living in Brighton to her liking, although she, like many new expats arriving for the first time in the United Kingdom, surprisingly discovered big differences between America and Britain.

"We expats like to say that the U.K. and the U.S. are 'two cultures separated by a common language.' Before I moved, I took for granted that living here would be a similar experience to living in America. After all, we do share a common language. I could not have been more wrong. In fact, I discussed this with a Polish friend of mine and I think she actually had an easier time with cultural adjustment because she prepared for the differences. Most Americans do not because they think it will be just like home."

The biggest differences she noticed were in the area of social protocol. Nicky is an introvert by nature and can be socially anxious, so it was not a big problem adjusting to the ways of the more reserved Brits. She still struggles, however, with picking up on the cultural nuances of conversations she has with locals.

Nicky has discovered that one of the joys of living in centuries-old England is a land suffused with history and culture at every turn. She makes sure that her children learn the heritage of their country.

"I like that there is so much culture in the United Kingdom for my children to grow up with. We do a lot of weekend trips to English Heritage National Trust sites, which include many famous historical sites around the U.K. You can visit castles, gardens, historic houses and ruins, like

Stonehenge, throughout the country. My daughter is just of the age where exposing her to these things will really benefit her. We are so fortunate that we are less than an hour from the great cultural treasures of London and just a short flight away from some of the world's greatest museums and other cultural attractions in Europe."

Everything Nicky cares about and cherishes is close at hand, except for her family and friends back home, which makes her sad because she has a very close relationship with her parents and brothers.

"I Skype with my mom and dad almost every day and they fly over here a couple of times a year, so that really helps, but it still is not enough for me. Mark and I flew back to visit my family four years ago when Madeline was an infant. Now, with two small children, making a long international flight is just too difficult for us."

Now that she has lived in England for over seven years, Nicky has developed strong opinions on life in her new country. One of the things that troubles her about living in the United Kingdom is the class disparity she has observed between the "haves and the have-nots." She thinks popular culture and the media accentuate the disparity.

"It seems to be pervasive in not only popular culture but also everyday conversation. There is always that sort of attitude amongst middle class families toward the working class and a distinct undertone of being better. There just seems to be a much more noticeable divide here than in America."

Climate often affects where expats put down roots, but Nicky is not bothered by the notoriously soggy southeastern England weather. She has found that Brighton's weather actually is a bit of an improvement over what she was used to in Ohio, with low temperatures seldom dipping below forty degrees Fahrenheit and snowfall negligible.

"The climate does not bother me at all, but it does bother a lot of other American expats who move here. I have looked at the weather statistics for Brighton and the Cincinnati area and they have about the same amount of rainfall days per year. The stereotype of rainy English weather is not as pronounced as everyone makes it out to be. Weather does not really bother me at all. I could live almost anywhere."

Although Nicky basically packed two suitcases and got on a plane for Brighton when she was just twenty-two, she highly recommends spending time researching the place you are moving to before you actually move there. She believes she would have been better prepared for the cultural differences if she had.

"I would say, 'do as I say, not do as I did.' I went on a few online groups and asked a few questions but that was about it. I have learned that you should become familiar with the laws of your new country. You should also know how living outside of the U.S. as an American citizen will impact you. For instance, as an American, I had lived here for several years before I realized that the Internal Revenue Service expected me to continue filing taxes. That is something you can and should research before you move."

Would she ever return to the U.S.? Nicky does not think so at this point in her life. There was a time in the first year or two when her feelings for living in Brighton were a little rocky, as a brand new expat. Now she thinks there are more opportunities for the family in England, especially since she has gained her British citizenship.

"At this time in our lives, especially with two little kids, we are looking to put down roots here in Brighton. Most of Mark's family is here, our business is here and our life is here. I want a solid foundation for my family and we are building it in Brighton. Perhaps once the kids are grown and have flown the nest and we make a million dollars, we might consider leaving Brighton. But if we do, it would be Europe, not America. I definitely could see us living on a nice little canal in Amsterdam."

CHAPTER 14

Rachel Chryczek
Age 22
Fagersta, Sweden

"Whenever I passed anyone, I would smile or make eye contact with them. In return, I would get blank stares, and sometimes it would look like a mean stare. It took me the longest time to realize that is just how Swedes are. It is not because they are mean or unfriendly, they are just very reserved."

RACHEL CHRYCZEK FOLLOWED her heart two years ago when she traded her small town in America's upper Midwest for Fagersta, Sweden, a few hours northwest of Stockholm. It has taken a while, but she is slowly putting smiles on the faces of her Nordic neighbors.

On the Saginaw River, less than two hours northwest of Detroit, Rachel's hometown of Bay City is a sleepy place of about thirty-five thousand people, including most of Rachel's family. She was born and raised there and seldom left, except for an occasional trip to see relatives in South Carolina and once to neighboring Canada.

Rachel's parents split when she was two and her mother, a registered nurse, remarried. Her dad passed away when she was just twelve.

After graduating from Bay City Central High School, Rachel enrolled in the town's local community college, Delta College, intent on studying for a bachelor's degree in psychology.

School went well, but as a young and sometimes bored digital-generation Millennial, she found herself drawn to online chat rooms for more social interaction. One day in 2008, she met Lenny from Sweden in one of the chat rooms she frequented.

"I cannot even tell you what chat room it was but Lenny and I talked for quite a few hours when we first met. Then we started emailing a lot and talking more until, four years later, we decided to meet in person for the first time."

Lenny was living in his hometown of Hallstahammar, Sweden, a small town of about eleven thousand people about an hour and a half northwest of Stockholm. Rachel flew to Sweden for the very first time in 2012, unsure of how her first meeting with Lenny would work out. She spent two weeks with Lenny and his family and knew then that she would return.

"We had communicated online and on Skype for four years, but after two years or so things started to turn romantic. I wanted to go to Sweden to make sure that the romance was real. When I flew back to Bay City, I knew it was."

Back home now, Rachel made the decision to leave her family, friends and college to move to Sweden and be with Lenny. Concerned about her education, though, Rachel spoke with her advisor at Delta College and was told she could take online classes to complete her studies.

"I knew that I could take only a few more classes with Delta, so I researched other online college options and found Southern New Hampshire University (SNHU), which is located in Manchester, New Hampshire. The university is a well regarded school and offers many degree programs and courses online."

Key to her decision to transfer to SNHU was the breadth of the psychology program the school offered. Rachel was looking for a degree program that had a concentration in addiction studies that went beyond just the traditional focus on alcoholism and drugs, but also included gambling, shopping, video games and other addictions. She also decided to add minors in sociology, which dovetailed nicely with her addiction-focused psychology degree, and professional writing, a new passion for her.

With her education plans now in place, Rachel set about preparing for her move to Sweden, which turned out to be a little harder than she initially thought.

"Probably the hardest thing for me to do was figure out what to pack. I bought a large suitcase that could hold about seventy pounds of clothes, and a duffel bag. I knew it was cold there and a lot more expensive, so I wanted to make sure I brought the right stuff. I am definitely an over-packer and had to keep repacking until I got it right."

Rachel found that getting a temporary visa to enter and live in Sweden was surprisingly simple and quick. When she returned to Bay City after her first visit to Sweden in May of 2012, she completed the required paperwork and filed her request for a temporary visa in August. To Rachel's surprise, her visa was approved in October. Although she had visa in hand, Rachel decided not to leave immediately, wanting to remain home for the holidays with her family and friends.

"I moved to Sweden on a temporary visa but I knew that I eventually would need a permanent residence card. There is no direct way to apply for permanent status, so you just apply for an extension of your temporary visa and the case- worker decides if they are going to grant you an extension or permanent status. I was finally granted permanent status, which now allows me to travel freely outside of the country. That was a weight off of my shoulders because I get homesick often and the temporary visa has more restrictions on how much time you can spend outside of Sweden. With my permanent card, I just have to renew it every five years."

With temporary visa in hand, Rachel left for Sweden in January of 2013. By this time, Lenny had moved to Fagersta, about an hour northwest of his hometown of Hallstahammar, to start a new job with an industrial baking company. The job did not last, though. The company decided to relocate its operations to Estonia and Lenny was laid off, although he spent several months training new Estonian workers after the move.

When Rachel arrived in Fagersta she was pleasantly surprised at its small town charm, even though it was the dead of winter.

"The town is actually really beautiful and has several large, clear lakes nearby. During the summer it is great to go water skiing and lie on the beach and just watch people. During the winter, just about everyone gets outdoors to hike in the forests and enjoy the snow, although it is not my favorite thing to do. I also like that Fagersta has only about eleven thousand people. It makes getting around very easy. We also like that we are just an hour from Lenny's family."

Rachel moved into Lenny's large one-bedroom apartment, a place he had rented when he first moved to Fagersta. She was not enthusiastic about it.

"It was absolutely the worst apartment ever but the only reason we were living there was Lenny had to get something quickly when he moved here. We stayed there for just a month before moving to our new apartment, which is on the second floor of a four-story building. It is a smaller place, but much nicer."

Rachel likes the location of her apartment, which is a quick five-minute drive or twenty-minute walk to the downtown area with its shops and restaurants.

"I go downtown often to shop and I must say that the biggest culture shock for me when I arrived was the stoicism of the Swedish people. It was hard for me to get used to smiling and saying hello to them and getting no response. I have never met a Swede who was not friendly, though, they just show it in a much different way. I am sure all American expats go through this."

She also had to get used to the daily "fika," a Swedish cultural habit of having coffee, often accompanied by pastries or sandwiches, similar to British teatime.

"I was not a huge coffee drinker when I lived at home but I like the custom now. It is more of a thing when we visit Lenny's family, especially his grandmother's house. She always has different cookies and cakes for us to eat with our coffee. And most people drink their coffee black here. When I drank coffee before, I would use special fun creamers. Not here."

She also has adjusted to the Swedish practice of shopping for food several times a week, rather than the weekly shopping she was used to in Bay City. Rachel admits that she ate too much fast food when she lived back home. She now shops often at the fresh food markets in Fagersta and prepares home-cooked meals most of the time.

"I am a picky eater and I am still not used to a lot of dishes prepared in Sweden. They love fish here and I must say that I have never been very big on fish. I do love the Swedish desserts, though. They have such a great variety of wonderful desserts, especially at Christmas."

Another disappointment for Rachel was the cost of almost everything in Sweden. She knew that things would be more expensive and the prices did not disappoint. After more than a year, she is finally used to Swedish prices and compensates by shopping less, since the couple is on a strict budget.

Rachel also found that she needed to adjust her thinking when it came to the hours retail stores were open in her small town.

"I was used to twenty-four-hour everything: gas stations, mini-marts, grocery stores and lots of other retail stores back home. Here, most things close by eight or nine in the evening. The local liquor store, for example, which is run by the state as a non-profit business, closes Saturdays and does not reopen until the following Monday."

Most of Rachel's cultural adaptation issues with Sweden are minor and she has been able to adjust quite easily, particularly with the help of Lenny, who has helped guide her through the cultural thicket.

"One of the things I must say that I do love about Sweden is the health-care system, which is part of the benefits of living here, even if you are a temporary resident. The state pays for everything except dental and eye care, which you have to pay out-of-pocket. Those costs are comparable to what I would have to pay in the U.S. I am quite happy overall with medical care, but I would prefer to have a personal physician that I could see all of the time. I had a bad experience with a doctor once who really rubbed me the wrong way. But because it is socialized medicine here, you do not get to have a personal physician. You see whatever doctor is available when you have an appointment. I really should not complain, though. Medical care is free, high quality and mostly everyone speaks English."

With Fagersta's bucolic setting and outdoor activities, the couple is on the go year-round, including spending every other weekend with

Lenny's family in nearby Hallstahammar, an hour away by car. Rachel looks forward to the drive, a winding two-lane road that passes through dark forests, translucent lakes and roaring rivers. She especially likes the peacefulness of the verdant rural landscape dotted with cows in meadows.

"It is one of my favorite things to do, especially now that we have a car and do not have to rely on public transportation. When I first moved here Lenny did not have his driver's license, which is typical in Europe since the public transportation systems are so good, even in small towns. I love that we can travel almost anywhere by bus and train if we want to."

As Rachel ventures outside of Fagersta more often, she has become aware of her lack of local language skills. She has had a problem communicating with Lenny's grandmother and father, who speak no English. That is a rarity in Sweden, which begins English language instruction in early primary school years.

"It is actually a problem that so many people speak English here. It makes it difficult to learn Swedish, which I will need competence in if I decide to apply for citizenship."

Soon after arriving in Fagersta, Rachel enrolled in a state-sponsored language program called Swedish for Immigrants (SFI). The program she took was taught locally and a big disappointment for her.

"We only met three days a week at the local high school for maybe three or four hours. I did not like the teacher at all, mainly because she took such an elementary, childish approach to learning Swedish. We colored, we sang and we played 'hangman' for a half hour at the end of each session. We did the same thing every time and it became monotonous. She really was not teaching us anything."

She was doubly disappointed when she learned that an American friend of hers, who lived about three hours away in a larger university town, had achieved Swedish language fluency in just several months.

"I think my problem had to do with living in such a small town with limited resources. Her SFI class was held at the university and they got to use computers to help them. She started in August and in a few short months was able to pass the national test for fluency. I gave up after week seven. Part of the problem was that I received my notice in the mail late and did not start the class until it had been underway for over two weeks, so I had to catch up. Since it was a total immersion class with no English spoken, I just got lost. Overall, it was a bad experience. I will try again, hopefully with better results."

She met her Swedish-fluent friend on an expat Facebook group, one of several Rachel frequents to connect with other Americans living in Sweden. Most live in the major cities of Stockholm, Malmö and Gothenburg.

"I have developed several relationships with other young women through the Facebook groups. Unfortunately, none of them live near me, although my friend who passed her national fluency test did come over for a weekend to visit when Lenny was out of town visiting with his brother. She is three years older than me and from Indiana. It was great to just sit around and listen to American music and talk with her. I really appreciated it because she lives three hours away."

Friends in Sweden help, but Rachel still gets homesick often and uses email, social media and Skype to stay close to her family.

"I typically call my grandma at least once a week and I try to reach out to my brother, but he is just fifteen, so it is a little difficult to keep a conversation going with him. I bought a subscription plan on Skype to call the U.S. with unlimited minutes and it allows me to call anyone, anytime. I also talk with my dad's sister, Aunt Dottie, who I am very close to. Staying in touch this way really helps but there is nothing like seeing them in person. We are planning a trip home to Bay City sometime this year."

After losing his job before Rachel arrived in Sweden, Lenny decided to enroll at Linköping University in Linköping, a small city of about one hundred thousand people located about two hours southwest of Stockholm.

"We will move at the end of the summer so Lenny can get started in his new program. One of the great things about Sweden is its higher education system, which is free not only for Swedish citizens, but also for permanent residents. He will also get student aid, which is equivalent to a grant in the U.S., which he does not have to pay back. I thought about going to university here, also, but instruction is strictly in Swedish and I am not there yet. I will stick with SNHU."

Lenny, who is five years older than Rachel, will not be done with his studies for about another three to five years. He will study environmental science on campus and also online. Rachel, on the other hand, will receive her diploma in 2017.

"I finished all of my Delta College classes online not long after I arrived in Sweden and I am now fully enrolled with SNHU. I am on track to graduate with my bachelor's degree in 2017. Once I graduate, I would love to work with teenagers and young adults who have experienced addiction themselves or have someone in their family with an addiction. My ultimate goal is to get a master's degree, but that will not be for a while."

With both attending university, marriage is not yet in their plans. The couple has decided to wait until they have more stable finances.

"We would like to get married after we both graduate. When that happens, we will probably move back to the States. We have talked about moving to Vermont or Maine, but at first we will move to Bay City because my family is there. Lenny would not have citizenship but he will get permanent resident status as my husband, which will allow him to work."

Although Rachel had adapted well and loves her expat life in Sweden, she wishes she had spent more time learning about the country before she moved.

"Once I decided to move, the process was very quick. I should have used the time to begin my Swedish lessons and learn more about the country. In retrospect, I think any expat should know something about the country's history, culture, money, climate and all of those other things that you will need to make the adjustment to living in a new land. Fortunately, I had Lenny to rely on, but I could have been a lot more prepared. There is so much to consider that I never thought of and should have."

CHAPTER 15

Megan Fitzgerald
Age 44
Singapore

"I have always had a passion for travel and different cultures ever since I could remember. When I was in the seventh grade, I started renting foreign films and taking French. That was how I started to see other parts of the world – through film."

THAT PASSION HAS led Megan Fitzgerald to Paris, London, Rome and now Singapore, where she operates her business, Career By Choice. As an expat and international career coach, she helps professionals and executives build and accelerate their careers abroad.

Megan got a taste of moving early in life. She was born in New York, but her father, an engineer for a major corporation, moved the family often.

"As a child I lived in New York, Pennsylvania, Virginia, Tennessee, Florida and Maryland. All of those moves probably helped me learn to adapt to new surroundings and inspired me to want to learn about new places."

After high school, Megan headed to Providence, Rhode Island where she attended the prestigious Ivy League school, Brown University. She got a degree in International Relations because she knew even then that she wanted to live and work internationally. She also got a degree in Semiotics – the study of how meaning is created. This allowed her the opportunity to see how meaning is constructed in different cultures and media, particularly film.

"When I was at Brown, I also spent a year in Paris. While in Paris, I was able to travel around France. After I finished my studies there I also was fortunate enough to travel all around Western and Eastern Europe. For me, exploring new countries and the international lifestyle was incredibly exciting."

After receiving her undergraduate degree in 1992, Megan headed south to Washington D.C., where she would spend the next ten years of her life. She started her career working for the United States Agency for International Development (USAID) in international education and training. She designed business training programs for entrepreneurs from developing and transitional economies in Africa, Asia, Latin America and Eastern Europe.

Early on during her time with USAID, Megan met Josh McCloud, her partner of 21 years and now her husband.

"We were very compatible. I think that one of the things that brought us together was our love of travel and other cultures. Josh's parents had been expats, so he grew up abroad. We made a conscious decision when we lived in Washington to move overseas and live a truly international lifestyle."

"After many years working in international education and training, I was able to design a master's degree in Multimedia Design and Communications at American University in Washington D.C. I was interested in leveraging multi-media and technology to facilitate international education, training and cultural exchange."

After she completed her master's degree, she took a job at an international arts organization, also based in Washington. Megan helped facilitate grants and did program development and organizational development for arts education organizations around the world.

"I did that for about a year. Josh and I had made a plan to move to London at that point, but right before we were about to leave I got cancer. So I stayed in the States to get cancer treatment while Josh left for London, having secured a job in a multinational IT company. As soon as my treatment was completed I joined him in London."

The couple then settled into the Marylebone area of London, an apartment on Baker Street, renowned as the fictional home of Sherlock Holmes.

"It was a real process to get a work permit in the United Kingdom and I ended up doing some consulting jobs with U.K. organizations. Knowing that London would just be a stop on our journey, the difficulty in getting that work visa was one of the motivations for starting my own business. I did not want to go through the work visa process every time we moved somewhere."

So after consulting for a few years in London, Megan decided to launch her new business, providing career coaching to expats.

"It made a lot of sense for my business to focus on helping expats because they tend to be very interesting, adventurous people and we had met so many of them in London. I could relate to their experience, understood their challenges and had been through many of the same unique challenges."

Megan and Josh loved their time in London with its diversity of restaurants and food, art and access to its museums and other cultural experiences, although Megan was not enthusiastic about the vagaries of London's weather. The beauty of the city and its cosmopolitan lifestyle and interesting people from all corners of the world had a strong hold on them. But their interest in other parts of the world inspired them to explore new places.

"After more than four years of living in London, we decided it was time for a change. Because I designed my business to be portable, I could live anywhere. As long as I had my laptop, Skype and an Internet connection I could literally work from wherever I wanted. And Josh also had a great deal of flexibility as far as where he could live since his company supported remote working. He just needed to be near a major international airport in Europe so that he could easily get to company and client meetings when necessary. So we began looking throughout Europe for a new place to call home."

After visits to many countries, Megan and Josh chose to live in Rome.

"Josh and I first made the decision to pursue going to London, and then we made the decision to go somewhere else, and chose Italy. All of our choices have been conscious choices. We knew where we were going, we knew what we wanted and we made plans to get there. This is not something that many expats have the luxury of doing."

"Rome is one of my favorite cities in the world, and I am really in love with Italy. I love everything about it: the culture, the food, the countryside, the architecture and the art."

Megan and Josh lived in Rome for more than six years, living first near one of Rome's largest piazzas, the Piazza del Popolo, and later in Monteverde Vecchio, a location less central, but their apartment had a wonderful view of the whole city.

Once settled in Rome, Megan continued her work in building a successful global, portable business.

"My education, training and skill set helped me develop a strong online presence when I first started my business. I wrote a lot of expert articles that helped create awareness for what I was doing, and then I got a big break about three years after I started when I was featured in a *Fortune* magazine article. It gave me lots of global visibility, which really helped put my business on the map. I also started a blog to promote my business and expertise."

She also is a popular speaker at forums and events specific to her business. Her speaking engagements have taken her all over the world but the majority of her relationships are built online. She is very active on social media and helps her expat clients build their online presence so they can achieve the level of what she calls "strategic visibility" to support building their international career.

Megan has worked with a wide range of global expat professionals and executives from over 45 countries who have between five and twenty-five years of professional experience.

"Usually they speak at least two languages and much of the time they are already living abroad as an expat on assignment looking to make a move. Sometimes they are still in their home country but want to build a career overseas."

Megan helps them clarify their career goals, develop unique value propositions and communicate their value propositions effectively, both online and offline. She also helps them build their strategic people network, one of the real keys to job success, and then helps them conduct an international job search. Most importantly, she shows them how to manage their international career for the long-term.

"I am definitely a high-touch kind of coach/consultant. I usually work with only eight or ten clients at a time to ensure that I provide that personal touch. I also sometimes do corporate work to support global executives as part of a leadership program."

After almost seven years in Rome, Megan and Josh started thinking about other locations that might offer them the same kind of expat lifestyle and enjoyment as Rome. Serendipitously in 2013, Josh received a job offer he simply could not turn down. It was based in Singapore, just off the southern tip of the Malay Peninsula where the Indian Ocean meets the South China Sea, just eighty-five miles north of the equator.

"Singapore was the only time that a job opportunity for Josh presented itself and we had to make the decision whether or not we wanted to move to Asia. We decided to take the job he had been offered because we had traveled a bit in Asia and really enjoyed ourselves. We wanted the opportunity to be able to explore more of Asia in depth."

One of the best things Megan loved about Singapore was its proximity to other countries and cultures. They could hop on a plane and spend a long weekend in many different places in Asia, like Thailand, which they have visited several times. The couple also has visited Nepal, Sri Lanka, Vietnam, Malaysia and Indonesia, and plan on much more travel to other Asian countries.

Megan and Josh found an apartment in the Robertson Quay area of Singapore, one of the quays along the Singapore River known for its café culture as well as proximity to many restaurants.

"One of the great things about living in Singapore, besides its central location for travel, is its wonderful diversity of food and people. The city is well known throughout the world as a top destination for 'foodies,' as well as its street food or 'hawker stalls' where you can sample food from a variety of Asian cultures very inexpensively. Both my husband and I really enjoy food and eating, so in this respect, Singapore is a great place for us."

Weather-wise, Singapore's location just north of the equator brings little variation in climate year-round, which is mostly hot and humid with about ninety-two inches of rain a year.

"The weather is probably the thing I like least about Singapore. It is around eighty degrees every day here. I do miss the seasons and being able to wear a nice warm sweater once in awhile."

Besides being a top business and financial center in Asia, there are several other reasons why expats enjoy Singapore, including its diverse and multicultural population. The majority population is Chinese, representing nearly seventy-five percent of all Singaporeans. Malays and Indians make up the second and third largest ethnic groups in the country. And since it is extremely safe and has great schools, it is a perfect place to raise a family.

Megan likes Singapore because, not only is it very clean and safe, everything is very well organized. It has a very modern, high-tech infrastructure, so almost everything can be done online. But things are changing somewhat in the world of employment in Singapore.

"Singapore historically has been built on the back of foreign talent. It has had very friendly visa programs that attracted skilled professionals and executives from around the world. Now, however, the government is putting in more policy protections to encourage companies to hire Singaporeans first. But those protection programs do not apply – at least at this point – to jobs that are over a certain salary level. So senior-level and executive jobs are still very much in reach for expats."

When Megan moved to Singapore, she had little trouble setting up her business, which took her just fifteen minutes to register online. She found that the experience was, thankfully, completely different from the bureaucracy she encountered while setting up her business in Italy.

One big plus for the couple has been the ease of integration into the local community, wherever they have been. Given their natural curiosity and experience with other cultures, Megan and Josh have not had any problems settling into their new homes.

"I would call it culture transition, not culture shock. I have trained and coached people on making cross-cultural career transitions all of my life, so I knew a lot about Asian culture before we arrived in Singapore. However, I can say that living in Asia has been more of a cultural transition than other places we have been."

Megan strongly believes that learning the local language is one of the key ways that expats can ease the transition into a new location.

"Learning the local language makes a big difference in most non-English-speaking places. I have decided, though, that I am not going to spend time learning Mandarin, mainly because the national language of Singapore is English. Mandarin is quite a challenge and not one that I am ready to take on at this time. In Italy, I was learning Italian because many of the people in Rome did not speak English or did not speak it well, so I was highly motivated to learn the language. It is also an incredibly beautiful language and really fun to speak."

One of the downsides Megan has found to living in Singapore is its distance from friends and family in the United States. It is twenty-nine hours door-to-door for Megan and Josh to visit family. And it is expensive. But visits home may not be as frequent now as the couple awaits their first child.

"We will be in Singapore for some time as we await the arrival of our new adopted child from the Republic of Marshall Islands. I do not think we will be picking up and moving any time soon because of the challenges of moving with an infant. But then again, who knows? Maybe we will have a child with a passion for travel, just like us."

Even with the arrival of their child, Megan plans to continue her business.

"I have been working since I was thirteen years old and I cannot imagine not working. I enjoy my work so much I would not want to stop. But I also want to enjoy motherhood. The beauty of my business is that I can scale it up or down as needed. So I may not be working as much when the child comes, but will most certainly continue to do what I am passionate about. One big help for us will be the cost of a nanny in Singapore, which is very inexpensive."

Now firmly established in Singapore, Megan loves to give advice to new expats, wherever they are headed. She advises expats to focus on integrating into their local communities as much as they can when they first arrive.

"I know that many new expats struggle to integrate. I tell them to get involved with the types of activities that allow you to meet the local people. Volunteering is a great way to do that and to also give back to your community. There are many ways to meet people. It is just a matter of getting over some of those social jitters that people experience."

Megan is quick to remind that she does not judge those expats who live in what are often called "expat ghettos." She believes there is no right answer for everyone.

"Many people really struggle to integrate when they move abroad, so if you want to live surrounded by other expats and it makes you happy, go with it."

Robert Nelson

Will Singapore be the end of the expat journey for Megan and Josh? Even with a new baby on the way, Megan thinks that, at some point, they may want to move closer to family, but still stay abroad.

"I am not sure when that might be, time will tell I guess. I think becoming parents will change our lives in big ways. My views will probably change as I spend some time being a mother. But as I often say, sometimes life happens while we are making other plans."

CHAPTER 16

Join the New American Expat Generation

ARE EXPATS DIFFERENT? Is there something in their DNA that causes them to pack their bags and leave family and friends of a lifetime to live in another country? Do they all have similar characteristics that set them apart from their homeland-bound peers? What does it take to be an expat?

All of the expats featured in the preceding chapters share a number of specific characteristics that have helped them join the new American expat generation and lead successful lives abroad. A little later in this chapter, each of our expats in this book will describe the characteristics most important to them.

But first, let us turn to an expert on the subject. Kelly Ross is an experienced leadership development and talent management expert who works primarily with expats. She worked for global consulting giant McKinsey & Company for ten years in twenty countries on three continents before opening her own Chicago-based consultancy.

While studying for her MBA at Northwestern University in 2011, Kelly did her graduate thesis on "The Characteristics of Successful Expatriates," by studying nearly two hundred expats living in seventy-three different countries. They were asked to assess their success as expats, both personally and professionally, and articulate what made them successful. Specifically, they were asked to determine the importance of five characteristics that had been judged, through qualitative research by Kelly, to be traits of a successful expat.

Kelly found that the number one characteristic an expat needs to possess is open-mindedness. What does that mean? It is your ability to look at your new environment with a desire to learn about and understand it and to see things differently. It means a willingness to try new methods and accept failure as a means to learn and improve. Expats told Kelly that being open to new and different practices, while accepting that there is not always a clear answer or direction, was critical to success.

Flexibility is a close second in Kelly's study, but many think it is the number one characteristic. It is your willingness to try new ways of doing things and be able to adapt to whatever situation might arise. If you are flexible, most other things are not quite so difficult. Adaptability, in most ways, is synonymous with flexibility.

The third most important characteristic is cultural sensitivity, defined as your ability to understand the culture in which you are living and working and integrate into it. Cultural sensitivity is showing an interest in your new culture, learning about it and accepting it. Expats spoke about cultural sensitivity in many different ways: "Interest in the new culture;" "curiosity and passion to learn new things culturally;" "the ability to fit into the new location and society;" and, "acceptance of my host culture for what it is."

Interestingly, adventurousness is the fourth most important characteristic. I say "interestingly" because research conducted by MyInternationalAdventure a few years ago showed that adventure was the number one motivator for younger Americans to move abroad. In Kelly's study, expats defined adventurousness as the desire to have exciting and new experiences, both at work and in life outside of work. Adventurousness did not come to mind for most expats at first, but when asked directly if it was important to success, ninety-five percent thought it was moderately or very important.

Adventurers Abroad

The final characteristic mentioned most by expats in Kelly's study is curiosity, defined as your interest in learning about your new culture, environment and job. One expat felt that curiosity was a "willingness to understand why things were being done."

Several of these characteristics also appeared in a list of attributes required for expat success prepared for MyInternationalAdventure by Erin Meyer. Erin is an affiliate professor of organizational behavior at the Paris campus of INSEAD, the international business school. She also is the author of *The Culture Map: Breaking Through the Invisible Boundaries of Global Business.* Erin specializes in cross-cultural management and spoke with me for an article published in 2014.

Erin's top five characteristics for successful expats include cultural understanding, flexibility, self-reliance, language skills and a sense of adventure. When it comes to her top choice, cultural understanding, she believes that expats need to learn how their new culture sees them, more than how expats view their new culture. She also places flexibility near the top because she believes expats need to be able to quickly adapt to any new situation that might arise.

Self-reliance is important because it helps push you to meet people and integrate more quickly. Language skills, often a weakness of American expats, allow you to live a much richer life in your new country by enabling you to fully integrate both socially and culturally. Finally, a strong sense of adventure helps lead people to explore far different cultures.

Although research and expert opinions help us understand the broader context of what it takes to be successful as an expat, I believe that the opinions that matter most come from the adventurers abroad in this book. I asked each of them to tell me what it takes to be successful living abroad.

"I think flexibility would be my first choice. I have found that many things do not go as planned when you move abroad. If you have a personality that requires control over everything, you are probably going to have a difficult time. I also think you need to be creative. You are not always going to find the things that you are used to having, whether that means food, household goods or other products. You need to be creative in how you cook, how you live your day-to-day life and how you manage situations that have never presented themselves before. You need to adapt."

Amanda Mouttaki
Marakesh, Morocco

"I think it is very important to have a good sense of who you are and be open to changing yourself. If you cannot, you will be finished. I also think flexibility is very important. It does not mean that you should give up who you are. You have to have a good sense of who you are initially and yet be willing to grow and change. You should also be open-minded. You must be able to dismiss your preconceived notions of what it was going to be like to live in your new place and embrace the reality of living there."

Heather Etchevers
Marseilles, France

"You definitely have to integrate yourself into the culture and force yourself out of your comfort zone. I met a lot of Americans and Canadians in Mexico who had lived in the country for many years but still did not speak Spanish. It is a sense of entitlement that you just have to get over. I meet expats from all over the world and they seem to integrate themselves better than most Americans. You have to stop comparing your new country with America and force yourself out of your comfort zone. It is absolutely the most important thing to do."

Tony Bishop
Buenos Aires, Argentina

"I think you need patience. Patience settling in, patience getting your Internet set up and patience getting your driver's license. Just a lot of patience for everything you encounter because it will be different. I would also say flexibility to roll with the punches, whatever they are, is also very important. Do not sweat the small stuff because you cannot change things anyway."

Lauren Kicknosway
Sydney, Australia

"You should definitely have a high cultural IQ to move abroad. I mean, by the time you become an expat, you need to have a mindset that accepts people for whom they are and not judge them, especially when it comes to race, religion and things like that. You are going to be in a whole different world. You need to become culturally adaptive and not be self-centered. The world does not revolve around you or America."

Laurat Ogunjobi
Manresa, Spain

"Definitely be adaptable. It is so easy to get a very concrete idea of another culture in your mind before you get there. When I moved to Japan I had preconceived ideas of what it would be like and had a difficult time getting used to the culture. You have to let go of your prejudices from the U.S. You have to let the experience change your mind. It is also very important to have humility. You cannot care if you are wrong. You have to be in the moment and then adapt to it."

Mathew Hatfield
Daigo, Japan

"Definitely open-mindedness. I think when you go to a new country you have to keep your mind open to new personal experiences. What you get out of it might not be what you thought about in the beginning, but be open to what it is and do not live in a bubble. I have found that being in a new place is a gift. It is almost like you get to start all over again, but in a way that you do not find in the States."

Whelma Cabanawan
Budapest, Hungary

"I think being open-minded is the most important characteristic. Understanding that it takes time to settle in a new place. It takes at least a year just to sort of get to grips with your new place and that can be very hard. I think a lot of people are unprepared for how difficult that is and how homesick they might end up. You should also know that the first year is probably going to be really, really hard, especially if you are not working. It helps to know ahead of time and be prepared for that. You should also have the ability to not take things seriously because when you are in a new culture and you do not really understand what is going on, you have to be able to laugh at yourself and stop worrying about it. Just letting that go helps a lot with adapting to your new surroundings."

Cordelia Rojas
Bangkok, Thailand

"I think that you have to be ready for anything, be flexible and adaptable to the local situation. We are used to things being very organized in the U.S. but that is not the case in Brazil, for example. You have to be ready to try new things and accept them. You also have to be curious about other people and other things. You can only learn by being curious."

Will Martinez
Rio de Janeiro, Brazil

"I think open-mindedness is the most important trait to have. You definitely need to be open-minded to step out of your comfort zone and be willing to try new things. If you are not open-minded, you will not have a very enjoyable time living in a new country. I am pretty reserved, so moving to Sweden forced me to get outside of my comfort zone. It makes it a lot easier to adjust to things. You also should not be afraid to ask questions that you think might make you sound stupid. Most people are very forgiving and appreciate that you are trying."

Rachel Chryczek
Fagersta, Sweden

"I think you really have to be self-reliant. A lot of people look for happiness and fulfillment externally but I think you have to realize that it really comes from within yourself. You have to be your own source of happiness on those days when you think it is not going to work out. Once you find that within yourself, it does not really matter where you live because all of the challenges you will find there are essentially the same no matter where you live."

Nicky Bryce-Sharron
Brighton, England

"I think that expats have to be very tolerant and patient. It can get very frustrating living abroad, especially trying to learn a new language and culture. You are not going to be able to integrate overnight, so do not get frustrated. Do not rush things."

Greg Webb
Cologne, Germany

"I think you have to be ready to accept changes in your life and be prepared for them, although it seems like you never really are. The most successful expats that I know look forward to new experiences and are eager to embrace them. Things will be a lot different from home, but do not spend your time complaining about them. Accept them for what they are and enjoy all those wonderful things that make your new home very special."

Jessica Sueiro
Curridabat, Costa Rica

"I think you have to understand that living and working in another culture adds a level of complexity and sometimes challenge to your life. If you welcome constant learning and being confused or uncertain about situations, then expat life is for you. One can say that living overseas is a romantic life but it really takes a certain type of person to embrace it and thrive in it. It is not for everyone. For those who are ready for the challenges of constant learning, it will be great. It is one of the things I love about being an expat. You are constantly learning new things. It is a very wonderful life and I would not trade it for the world."

Megan Fitzgerald
Singapore, Singapore

All of our adventurers abroad share many of the characteristics that define and shape a successful modern-day expatriate, and today lead happy and fulfilling lives in their new countries. Would you like to join them? Do you have what it takes to be part of the new American expat generation?

If you would like more information on expat life, or would just like to reach out and connect with me, contact me at bob@myinternationaladventure.com. I am looking forward to hearing from you new Adventurers Abroad.

About the Author

AN EXPAT FOR nearly seven years in the Mexican tropical paradise of Puerto Vallarta, Mexico, Robert Nelson is the author of *Boomers in Paradise: Living in Puerto Vallarta*. He has also lived in Germany, Turkey and Greece and has traveled to over a dozen countries on three continents.

After operating his global brand consulting business in Puerto Vallarta, he returned to the San Francisco Bay Area several years ago to resume teaching advertising to the Millennial generation at San Jose State University

He then combined his more than forty years of marketing, communications, media and teaching experience with his expat knowledge and insights to launch the online guide myinternationaladventure.com with his wife, Felice, in 2013.

Acknowledgements

FELICE ARDEN NELSON, Dennis Green and Julie K. Rose for their long hours reading and editing each page of this book.

San Jose State University students Michelle Li and Sarah Ybarra for assisting me in researching the Introduction and Chapter One, and transcribing expat interviews.

Sources

Introduction

1. United Nations Department of Economic and Social Affairs Population Division. "International 2013 Migration." 2013.
2. Green, Nancy. "Expatriation, Expatriates, and Expats: The American Transformation of a Concept." *American Historical Review*, 2009.
3. U.S. Department of State, Bureau of Consular Affairs. "Who We Are and What We Do: Consular Affairs by the Numbers." 2013.
4. Costanzo, Joe and Klekowski von Koppenfels, Amanda. "Counting the Uncountable: Overseas Americans." Migration Policy Institute, 2013.

Chapter 1

1. MyInternationalAdventure LLC. "MyInternationalAdventure Segmentation Study." 2011.
2. U.S. Department of State, Bureau of Consular Affairs. "Who We Are and What We Do: Consular Affairs by the Numbers." 2013.
3. Institute of International Education. "Open Doors." 2014.
4. New Global Initiatives. "Expat Surveys." 2005 – 2011.
5. i-World Research. "Expat Survey 2013." 2014.
6. Deloitte LLP. "The Deloitte Millennial Survey." 2014.
7. Pricewaterhouse Coopers (PwC). "PwC's NextGen: A Global Generational Study." 2013.

8. U.S. Department of State. "Private American Citizens Residing Abroad." 2013.

Chapter 15

1. Ross, Kelly. "Characteristics of Successful Expatriates: Unleashing Success by Identifying and Coaching on Specific Characteristics." Northwestern University, 2011.

Made in the USA
San Bernardino, CA
22 December 2016